Song of Karmapa

Song of Karmapa

The Aspiration of the Mahamudra of True
Meaning
by Lord Rangjung Dorje

A Commentary by

Chökyi Nyima Rinpoche

Foreword by His Eminence Tulku Urgyen
Rinpoche

Translated by Erik Pema Kunsang
Edited by Marcia Binder Schmidt

Rangjung Yeshe Publications
Kathmandu

RANGJUNG YESHE PUBLICATIONS
FLAT 2B GREENVIEW GARDEN
125 ROBINSON ROAD, HONG KONG

RANGJUNG YESHE PUBLICATIONS
KA-NYING SHEDRUB LING MONASTERY
P.O. BOX 1200, KATHMANDU, NEPAL

COPYRIGHT © 1992 CHÖKYI NYIMA RINPOCHE
COPYRIGHT © ROOT VERSES 1988 ERIK HEIN SCHMIDT

FIRST EDITION, 1992

ALL RIGHTS RESERVED. NO PART OF THIS BOOK MAY BE REPRODUCED WITHOUT WRITTEN PERMISSION FROM THE PUBLISHER.

PRINTED IN THE UNITED STATES OF AMERICA

PUBLICATION DATA:

>CHÖKYI NYIMA RINPOCHE (B. 1951). FOREWORD BY HIS EMINENCE TULKU URGYEN RINPOCHE (B. 1920).
>SONG OF KARMAPA TRANSLATED FROM THE TIBETAN BY ERIK PEMA KUNSANG (ERIK HEIN SCHMIDT). EDITED BY MARCIA BINDER SCHMIDT 1ST ED.
>ISBN 962-7341-14-2 (PBK.)
>1. BUDDHIST MEDITATION. 2. MAHAMUDRA. 3. VAJRAYANA PHILOSOPHY. 4. KARMAPA—KAGYü. 5. BUDDHISM—TIBET. I. TITLE.

ASSOCIATE EDITOR: KERRY MORAN
COVER DESIGN BY JOSJE POLLMAN AND BRIGID RYAN
COVER DRAWING BY KONCHOK LHADRIPA

SONG OF KARMAPA IS BASED ON THE ASPIRATION OF THE MAHAMUDRA OF TRUE MEANING, A SONG WRITTEN BY THE THIRD KARMAPA, RANGJUNG DORJE.

TABLE OF CONTENTS

Proclamation by His Holiness the 16th Karmapa 9

Root verses 11

Foreword by Tulku Urgyen Rinpoche 17

Introduction 20

The Support 25

The Unmistaken Way 44

No Contradictions 63

Cutting through Misconceptions 78

Experience and Realization 89

Unity 106

Perfection 118

Appendix: Outline by Situ Pema Nyinchey 127

ACKNOWLEDGEMENTS

We would like to thank our Dharma friends who donated their time and talents to this book. At the request of Ben Rosensweig these teachings were given by Chökyi Nyima Rinpoche in the summer of 1986 at Ka-Nying Shedrub Ling Monastery, Boudhanath, Nepal. Ben carried out the transcribing of the recorded tapes with S. Lhamo. The rough editing was done by Judith Amtzis and Belinda Coulstock. The manuscript was finely tuned by Kerry Moran and proofread by several friends. Please excuse the omission of a detailed glossary; if necessary, the reader can refer to Rinpoche's earlier books. We would especially like to thank Rinpoche for offering such enlightened teachings and for allowing the book to be published.

Erik and Marcia
Schmidt

DEDICATION

The endeavor of explaining, scrutinizing, and composing this book has been undertaken with the wish that all sentient beings may realize the ultimate natural state, the innate wakefulness that is Mahamudra.

Chökyi Nyima Rinpoche

HIS HOLINESS
THE GYALWA KARMAPA

DHARMA CHAKRA CENTRE
RUMTEK
GANGTOK
SIKKIM

PROCLAMATION TO ALL FAITHFUL PEOPLE WHOSE EYES ARE WIDE OPEN TO THE DHARMA

This is to certify that I have recognized Drongtrül Chökyi Nyima Rinpoche as the seventh incarnation of the Dharma sovereign of Drong-ngur Tubten Shedrub Dargye Ling Monastery. From the age of thirteen, he has studied here at my seat, Rumtek Monastery, reflecting upon an ocean of scriptures. Like filling a vase to the brim, I have personally bestowed upon him empowerments, reading transmissions, and oral instructions.

In accordance with my command, the eminent Tulku Urgyen Rinpoche, my root guru, has established a new institute for the Buddhadharma in the country of Nepal. For that reason, with an auspicious enthronement, I have reinstated Chökyi Nyima Rinpoche in his traditional position of a superior incarnate lama of the Kagyü lineage.

Having empowered him as an upholder of the Buddhadharma, he shall be capable of benefitting living beings and spreading the teachings. This he shall do by safekeeping and sustaining the Dharma and by means of exposition, debate and composition, in that monastery as well as in all countries worldwide. It is my deepest aspiration that this may be accomplished.

This was written by the sixteenth in the line of incarnations of the glorious Karmapas on the tenth of September, 1974, at the great monastery of Rumtek in Sikkim (India).

THE MAHAMUDRA ASPIRATION OF TRUE MEANING

Namo guru.

All masters and yidam deities of the mandalas,
Victorious ones and spiritual sons throughout the three times and ten directions,
Pay heed to me and bestow your blessings
That I may attain accomplishment in accordance with my aspirations.

Springing forth from the snow mountain of the pure thoughts and deeds
Of myself and all countless beings,
May streams of virtue, undefiled by the threefold concepts,
Flow into the ocean of the four kayas of the victorious ones.

For as long as we have not attained that,
May we, throughout our succession of lives and rebirths,
Never even hear the words misdeeds or suffering,
But enjoy this splendorous ocean of happiness and virtue.

Song of Karmapa

*Having obtained the supreme freedoms and riches,
  possessing faith, endcavor and intelligence,
We have followed an eminent spiritual guide and
  received the nectar of oral instructions.
Without any obstacles for accomplishing them correctly,
May we, in all our lives, practice the sacred teachings.*

*By learning the scriptures and through reasoning we
  are freed from the veil of ignorance.
Through contemplating the oral instructions we
  overcome the darkness of doubt.
With the light resulting from meditation we illuminate
  the natural state as it is.
May the light of this threefold knowledge increase.*

*Through the nature of the ground, the two truths free
  from the extremes of eternalism and nihilism,
And the supreme path, the two accumulations free from
  the limits of exaggeration and denigration,
We attain the fruition of the two benefits free from the
  extremes of existence and peace.
May we connect with such a teaching free from error.*

*The ground of purification is mind essence, the union
  of being empty and cognizant.
That which purifies is the great vajra-like practice of
  Mahamudra.
May we realize the immaculate dharmakaya — the
  fruition of having purified
All the passing stains of confusion, that are to be
  purified.*

*To have cut misconceptions of the ground is the
  confidence of the view.
To sustain that undistractedly is the key point of
  meditation.*

Song of Karmapa

To train in all the points of practice is the supreme action.
May we possess the confidence of view, meditation and action.

All phenomena are the illusory display of mind.
Mind is devoid of 'mind' — empty of any entity.
Empty and yet unceasing, it manifests as anything whatsoever.
Realizing this completely, may we cut its basis and its root.

We have mistaken our nonexistent personal experience to be the objects,
And by the power of ignorance, mistaken self-cognizance to be a 'self.'
This dualistic fixation has made us wander in the sphere of samsaric existence.
May we cut ignorance and confusion at the very root.

It is not existent since even the victorious ones do not see it.
It is not nonexistent since it is the basis of samsara and nirvana.
This is not a contradiction, but the Middle Way of unity.
May we realize the nature of mind, free from extremes.

Nothing can illustrate it by the statement, "this is it."
No one can deny it by saying, "This is not it."
This nature transcending concepts is unconditioned.
May we realize this view of true meaning.

Without realizing this, we circle through the ocean of samsara.
When realizing it, buddhahood is not somewhere else.
It is completely devoid of "it is this" or "it is not this."
May we see this vital point of the all-ground, the nature of things.

Song of Karmapa

Perceiving is mind, being empty is also mind.
Realizing is mind, being mistaken is also mind.
Having arisen is mind, having ceased is also mind.
May we cut through all our doubts concerning mind.

Unspoiled by intellectual and deliberate meditation,
And unmoved by the winds of ordinary distractions,
May we be skilled in sustaining the practice of mind essence,
Being able to rest in unfabricated and innate naturalness.

The waves of gross and subtle thoughts having spontaneously subsided,
The river of unwavering mind naturally abides.
Free from the stains of dullness, sluggishness and conceptualization,
May we be stable in the unmoving ocean of shamatha.

When looking again and again into the unseen mind,
The fact that there is nothing to see is vividly seen as it is.
Cutting through doubts about its nature being existent or nonexistent,
May we unmistakenly recognize our own essence.

When observing objects, they are seen to be the mind, devoid of objects.
When observing the mind, there is no mind, as it is empty of an entity.
When observing both, dualistic fixation is spontaneously freed.
May we realize the natural state of the luminous mind.

Being free from mental fabrication, it is Mahamudra.
Devoid of extremes, it is the Great Middle Way.

Song of Karmapa

It is also called Dzogchen, the embodiment of all.
May we attain the confidence of realizing all by knowing one nature.

Great bliss, free from attachment, is unceasing.
Luminosity, devoid of fixation, is unobscured.
Nonthought, transcending the intellect, is spontaneously present.
Without effort, may our experience be unceasing.

The fixation of clinging to good experiences is spontaneously freed.
The confusion of "bad thoughts" is naturally purified.
Ordinary mind is free from acceptance and rejection.
May we realize the truth of dharmata, devoid of constructs.

The nature of all beings is always the enlightened state.
But, not realizing it, they wander endlessly in samsara.
Towards the countless sentient beings who suffer,
May overwhelming compassion arise in our minds.

The play of overwhelming compassion being unobstructed,
In the moment of love the empty essence nakedly dawns.
May we constantly practice, day and night,
This supreme path of unity, devoid of errors.

The eyes and superknowledges resulting from the power of practice,
The ripening of sentient beings, the cultivation of buddha realms,
And the perfection of aspirations to accomplish all enlightened qualities —
May we attain the buddhahood of having accomplished ripening, cultivation, and perfection.

Song of Karmapa

*By the power of the compassion of the victorious ones
   and their sons in the ten directions
And by all the perfect virtue that exists,
May I and all beings attain accomplishment in
   accordance with these aspirations.*

This aspiration, the Mahamudra of true meaning, was written by Lord Karmapa Rangjung Dorje.

FOREWORD

Here I will briefly discuss the life of the third Karmapa, since Dudjom Rinpoche offers a more detailed explanation of the Karmapa lineage in his *History of the Dharma*. Many lifetimes ago, when the first Karmapa attained enlightenment, the dakinis presented him with a black crown made from the hair of one hundred thousand dakinis. This was a sign that the Karmapa embodies the enlightened activity of the buddhas. 'Karma' means activity, and 'Karmapa' means 'the one who carries out the activity of all the buddhas'. By so doing, the Karmapa's unceasing stream of emanations are all amazingly wonderful.

The first Karmapa, Düsum Khyenpa, was a disciple of Gampopa, the chief holder of Milarepa's lineage. After Düsum Khyenpa passed away, he reincarnated in human form through the power of his desire to benefit all beings. The second Karmapa, Karma Pakshi, was the first recognized tulku in Tibetan history. As a small boy he met his chief student, Drogön Rechen. Proclaiming "I am Karmapa, the world-renowned one," he related all the details of his former incarnation to his astonished disciple.

Karma Pakshi was invited to teach the Emperor of China, who gave him the title Supreme Dharma Master. The Emperor, himself the incarnation of a bodhisattva, by means of his clairvoyance saw the black wisdom crown that is inseparable from the wisdom body of the Karmapas. He asked permission to make a crown resembling this subtle wisdom crown, so that ordinary beings could also have the fortune of seeing it. Since then all the Karmapas have worn the black crown as their distinctive emblem. There are many stories about people who are able to see the Karmapa wearing the two crowns. One such person is the present Dalai Lama, Tendzin Gyatso, who once told the 16th Karmapa, "You have taken off one crown, but still wear another!"

After Karma Pakshi passed away, his incarnation was conceived in the womb of an unmarried woman. People in the area believed that an illegitimate birth would surely bring hailstorms to destroy their crops, and it was the custom to banish the mother before the birth. Full of shame and without telling anyone of her pregnancy, the woman fled to the upper part of the valley. After secretly giving birth to a boy, she placed the infant on the ground and buried him beneath a heap of large rocks. As she was about to leave, she heard a voice from under the stones saying, "Mother! You missed a small opening. I can still see the stars!" She covered the hole and left. A day or two later she thought, "A newborn child who can talk must be either an evil apparition or very wonderful. I will go back and see!" One week had passed by the time she reached the place where she had buried the child. She found the small Rangjung Dorje lying singing vajra songs. It was later said that in this world only two beings have been born totally free from the 'obscuration of the womb': Buddha Shakyamuni and Rangjung Dorje.

After the second Karmapa, Karma Pakshi, died, no one searched for his reincarnation. The small boy who was the third Karmapa simply told his mother, "My monastery is that way. Take me there!" So after many days' travel, mother and child reached a place where Tsurphu could be seen across a river. The small Karmapa immediately began to dance and cry out, "Mother! There is my monastery! I am so happy, so delighted!" One can still see some twenty footprints that

Song of Karmapa

his three-year-old body left in the rock. He was like the Buddha.

The teachings of the third Karmapa, Rangjung Dorje, have been transmitted through an unbroken lineage to the sixteenth Karmapa. Rangjung Dorje was an indispensable lineage master for the Dzogchen teachings. He and Longchen Rabjam shared the same teacher, Rigdzin Kumararaja, and also taught one another. Longchenpa himself clarified numerous difficult points with Rangjung Dorje, his Dharma brother. Thus, in the Dzogchen lineage, the one who is renowned as 'Omniscient Longchenpa, Matchless Throughout the Three Worlds' was himself Rangjung Dorje's disciple.

Although Rangjung Dorje was a Kagyü he was also an important master in the Nyingma lineage. In a vision in which Vimalamitra dissolved into the place between his eyebrows, Rangjung Dorje received the teachings now called Karmey Nyingtig and was endowed with the ability to transmit the entire Nyingtig system of Ati Yoga. He was a most wondrous master.

It is believed that Rangjung Dorje wrote *The Aspiration of Mahamudra* on the shore of the great ocean on his journey through China at the invitation of the Chinese emperor. *The Aspiration* not only expresses the meaning of Mahamudra but encompasses all three of the great views: Madhyamika, Mahamudra, and Dzogchen. Its profundity is difficult to match.

Karma Pakshi, the second Karmapa, wrote down the names of his subsequent twenty incarnations. From that time none of the Karmapas has had to be named. Karma Pakshi's immediate successor was Rangjung Dorje, the fourth Karmapa was Rölpey Dorje, and so forth. Every incarnation in the lineage holds the name which Karma Pakshi gave, and at the present time a name awaits the coming reincarnation.

Spoken by Tulku Urgyen Rinpoche

INTRODUCTION

The teaching called *The Aspiration of the Mahamudra of True Meaning* was composed by the third Karmapa, Lord Rangjung Dorje. It is called 'aspiration' but in fact it is a succinct instruction on Mahamudra. When you read it or chant it, this aspiration points out the realization of the ultimate transmission, your innate wakefulness that is Mahamudra, exactly as it is.

It is my wish that the reader pay close attention to both the words and the meaning, taking them to heart and applying them personally. Reading the aspiration in this way will activate the wisdom of realization within your being, facilitating the recognition of the authentic view. For the practitioner who has already recognized the view of Mahamudra, chanting this aspiration will enhance the view and infuse you with the blessings of the lineage. There are many reasons to chant this extraordinary aspiration.

I received this teaching from the sixteenth Karmapa. Pawo Rinpoche who has a very close lineage from Rangjung Dorje, gave me the reading transmission and was kind enough to clear up some questions I had. In addition, I received the transmission and some teachings from Tulku Urgyen Rinpoche as well as Kunu Lama Tendzin Gyatso.

The Aspiration of Mahamudra belongs to Buddhism's third vehicle, the Vajrayana. Of the two Vajrayana paths, the path of means and the path of liberation, Mahamudra belongs to the path of liberation. This aspiration, which very clearly states the key points of Mahamudra, possesses great blessings and profound meaning. For those who have not yet recognized the view, it offers instructions on understanding Mahamudra, while for those who have recognized the view, it offers instructions on enhancement. In itself, this song is an unexcelled and profound instruction, complete and without error.

The root verses of *The Aspiration of the Mahamudra of True Meaning* can be divided into three parts. First is the basis or support for making the aspiration. The second part contains the teachings introducing Mahamudra, and the third part or conclusion contains the dedication of merit and the making of good wishes.

Whenever we approach this teaching we should embrace the motivation of the greater vehicle of Mahayana, engendering the thought, "I will try to establish all sentient beings, as many as the sky is vast, in the state of perfect buddhahood endowed with the four kayas and the five wisdoms."

Keep the following in mind: throughout our innumerable past lives, each of these beings has at some time been mother, father, sister and brother to us. Although these beings who are 'our former mothers' wish for happiness, they do not know how to create virtuous actions which are the cause for happiness. Overcome by ignorance and disturbing emotions, sentient beings automatically engage in nonvirtue and create their own suffering. Thus they continually circle in samsara.

Think of the kindness bestowed upon us by our 'old mother sentient beings,' not only our present mother but also those of former lives. Think of the difficulties a mother endures. Consider a mother's great kindness and love for her child. She cares for it in every possible way, providing the best food, clothing and shelter. She continually regards her precious child as more important than herself.

Song of Karmapa

By realizing that all sentient beings have been our own mothers, in the past and by seeing how now they create only suffering for themselves, we cannot help feeling tremendous compassion and wonder how we can liberate them. To accomplish this, we need to engage in Dharma practice ourselves.

Merely studying Dharma teachings is not sufficient. We must think about them, examine the information thoroughly, and clear away any doubts which exist in our minds. Most importantly, we must put the teachings into practice through meditation. By doing so we will be able to realize the natural state of Mahamudra in this very lifetime and thus attain the level of complete enlightenment. Accomplishing this state, we will be capable of benefiting all beings.

When engaging in Dharma practice the vital point to understand is ultimate truth. Many have realized this in the past through coming into contact with a qualified master and receiving the pointing-out instruction. This transmission can occur in various ways. In past times, a qualified master and student merely sat together and let their minds mingle, engendering understanding in the student. Transmission was also accomplished by a simple gesture or sign. Nowadays, communication through words is of the utmost importance, and this communication entails personal study.

Study is essential because it is through studying the teachings that we clear away the obscurations which cause us to deviate from the path. We must study in order to get rid of misconceptions about the ultimate truth. Then, through reflection upon the meaning, we free ourselves from doubt. Finally, through meditation, we experience our innate wisdom.

There is so much we can study and learn. There are the extensive teachings known as the Tripitaka — the three collections comprised of the Vinaya, Abhidharma, and Sutra — as well as the profound teachings, the four tantras called Kriya, Charya, Yoga and Anuttara. All these different levels of teachings appear through the skillful means and great compassion of the buddhas and are taught in order to benefit different types of people.

For people living in this present age in which the five degenerations are rampant, the Vajrayana teachings are especially suitable. The key point in Vajrayana practice is to acknowledge that buddhahood, the state of enlightenment, is not something to search for elsewhere. It is not a place to reach or a thing to acquire. Buddhahood is actually the basic state that we already possess, the wisdom dwelling within. Innate wakefulness, dharmakaya, the body of wisdom qualities, merely needs to be uncovered. The Buddha is already within oneself.

Although this state of enlightenment is our natural possession, at present it is hidden by obscurations. By practicing the Hinayana and Mahayana teachings certain layers of obscurations will be purified and vanish, and various levels of attainment will arise corresponding to the degree of purification. These are the various stages of the shravakas, and bodhisattva paths.

According to the Mahayana system, the obscuration of disturbing emotions is totally purified at the first bhumi; however, the more subtle obscuration of habitual tendencies still exists. As these defilements continue to be cleared away we progress through the subsequent bhumis until, at the seventh bhumi, only the most subtle obscuration of dualistic knowledge remains. At the end of the tenth bhumi this obscuration is totally eliminated through the vajra-like samadhi, and the state of complete enlightenment is uncovered.

Compared to this stage-by-stage progression, the Vajrayana approach is much more subtle and profound. It focuses on the recognition of the correct view, the wisdom inherent within oneself. This recognition can occur when a qualified student, having become a suitable recipient, comes into contact with a qualified master.

Song of Karmapa

The Buddha gave 84,000 different Dharma teachings and countless commentaries have been written about them. Yet when we condense these vast numbers of teachings and commentaries into their quintessence, the message is simply that we should realize our basic wakefulness, our innate self-existing wisdom. We must receive instructions on how to remove the obscurations preventing realization of our own buddha nature. The essential substance expressed in Dharma teachings is really nothing more than this.

Milarepa said, "Fooling yourself with the vehicles of expedient meaning, you lose the chance to realize the inherent buddha." If we spend all of our time studying and contemplating only the expedient teachings, the relative truth, we do not find the opportunity to realize the true, definitive meaning. The essence of the Dharma teachings is discovered through the knowledge which results from meditation. Through mere intellectual study and conceptual understanding, we fail to realize directly that the 'buddha' is already inherent in ourselves. Words and concepts alone cannot clear away the obscurations concealing our inherent buddha nature. If we concentrate strictly on the superficial aspects of the Dharma teachings we are fooling ourselves. All our endeavors take on the aspect of a game.

Although the 84,000 Dharma teachings encompass an incredible amount of material, *The Aspiration of Mahamudra* condenses them all into a very clear, concise and effective instruction. It has few words but profound meaning, and is very beneficial. It is incredible — the king of all aspirations.

1

THE SUPPORT

Namo guru.

The *Aspiration of Mahamudra* begins with Sanskrit: "Namo Guru." Namo means 'I pay homage to,' and Guru means 'master.' Without a master, a teacher who gives us the oral pointing-out instruction, we cannot realize Mahamudra, the natural state of mind. It is because of this personal connection and presence that the master is considered very precious.

All masters and yidam deities of the mandalas,
Victorious ones and spiritual sons throughout the three
    times and ten directions,
Pay heed to me and bestow your blessings
That I may attain accomplishment in accordance with
    my aspirations.

This first verse engenders the support for the *Aspiration*, the persons before whom we make the aspiration. This support includes all the masters who have given us empowerment, reading transmission or oral instructions, as well as all the masters of the three lineages. The yidam deities are the buddha aspects of the different mandalas, such as Chakrasamvara, Vajra Yogini or Gyalwa Gyamtso, with whom we have made a

Song of Karmapa

karmic link by tossing the flower during an empowerment. The victorious ones are the buddhas of the ten directions and the three times. Their spiritual sons are the bodhisattvas as well as the shravakas and the pratyekabuddhas. We ask that they kindly pay heed to us and bestow their blessings so that we may 'attain the accomplishment' of the Mahamudra of true meaning as explained in the text.

*Springing forth from the snow mountain of the pure
    thoughts and deeds
Of myself and all countless beings,
May streams of virtue, undefiled by the threefold
    concepts,
Flow into the ocean of the four kayas of the victorious
    ones.*

Now the actual aspiration begins. When someone is practicing the Dharma, be it yourself, your Dharma friends or other sentient beings, purity of both thought and deed is needed. Purity of thought, however, is most important. If intentions are pure then deeds will also be pure.

We can gain some insight into purity of thought from the story of a hermit practitioner in Tibet named Geshe Ben. Being a devout practitioner he usually arranged his shrine neatly. One day, because his sponsor was coming, he made it especially nice. When he reflected on the extra care he was taking, he found that he was actually doing it only to show off, in order to possibly get more donations from his benefactor. Seeing his hypocrisy and realizing that his motivation was not in accord with the teachings, he took a handful of ashes and scattered them on his shrine, making quite a mess. Phadampa Sangye, who was in Tibet at that time, heard this story later and said, "People make offerings and place water bowls on shrines in many places in Tibet, but when Geshe Ben threw ashes on his shrine he made the most excellent offering. He had the most noble

Song of Karmapa

thought and action. Make offerings as he did." This may sound funny since throwing dirt on the shrine is usually considered an impure offering, but Geshe Ben's pure motivation was more important than the physical act.

Snow mountains, which are very white and immaculate and never black, are used to symbolize purity of thought and deed. Likewise the pure water flowing from these snow mountains is compared to streams of virtue. Based on the pure motivation and actions of body, speech and mind, different types of virtue are accumulated: meritorious virtue with focus, wisdom virtue beyond focus, the virtue of abandoning the ten unvirtuous actions and the virtue of observing the precepts of individual liberation, bodhisattva vows and tantric samayas.

Pure or undefiled accumulation of virtue depends upon both means and knowledge and these two should never be separated. Whatever the amount of your virtue, it should be suffused with knowledge and means united. In that way it will be pure virtue. Without both knowledge and means there is no ultimate benefit; buddhahood will not be attained. With knowledge but no means, or with means and no knowledge, enlightenment will take a long time. When these two are separated the virtuous action is said to be defiled, like a muddy stream of water from which no one wants to drink.

According to the general teachings, one practices by always acting with threefold purity, the unity of emptiness and compassion. Any act grounded in emptiness has this threefold purity, meaning that it is free from the concepts of subject, object, and action. An action free from these three concepts is pure or undefiled. Even a virtuous action is defiled when linked to the three concepts.

The ocean of the four kayas of the victorious ones refers to the enlightened state. No water is lost in this world because all the rivers flow into the great ocean. Likewise, by embracing the rivers of your actions with the threefold purity, they can flow no other way than into the vast ocean of the four kayas: dharmakaya, sambhogakaya, nirmanakaya and svabhavikakaya.

For as long as we have not attained that,
May we, throughout our succession of lives and rebirths,
Never even hear the words 'misdeeds' or 'suffering,'
But enjoy this splendorous ocean of happiness and
virtue.

"For as long as we have not attained that" refers to the four kayas of enlightenment, the unsurpassed state of buddhahood which is the absence of all defects and the perfection of all good qualities. This enlightened state is endowed with the two kinds of supreme knowledge: knowing the nature as it is and perceiving all that exists. The enlightened state also possesses the compassion of love and the activities of enlightened deeds. For as long as we have not attained that, may we, throughout our succession of lives and rebirths, never even hear the words 'misdeeds' or 'suffering', much less engage in them.

From the cause, which is misdeeds and disturbing emotions, comes the result, unhappiness and the three kinds of suffering. Without cause there will be no result. The causes for happiness and well-being are virtuous actions. By refraining from evil deeds and acting virtuously, may our enjoyment of happiness and virtue be boundless like an ocean.

Having obtained the supreme freedoms and riches,
possessing faith, endeavor and intelligence,
We have followed an eminent spiritual guide and
received the nectar of oral instructions.
Without any obstacles for accomplishing them correctly,
May we, in all our lives, practice the sacred teachings.

To be able to practice the teachings we need the proper support of the precious human body, defined as possessing the eight freedoms and the ten riches. Having the eight freedoms basically means having leisure, the freedom to practice the Dharma unfettered by the eight unfree states. These eight unfree states are to be born in the three lower realms, in the god realms, as a human with wrong views, as a savage, with incomplete senses or in a place where a buddha has not appeared.

Why are these states unfree? The intense pain and suffering of the lower realms precludes concentration on Dharma practice. In the hells one suffers from heat and cold, in the realm of the hungry ghosts from thirst and hunger, and in the animal realm from slavery and stupidity. In the higher realms there is too much pleasure. The gods and demigods suffer from pride, jealousy, ill-will and enjoyable distractions. Absorbed by their pleasure and antagonism, they do not even consider engaging in Dharma practice.

The human realm is somewhere in between, with both pleasure and pain. Humans experience the pain of birth, aging, falling sick and dying. There are also many other types of suffering, such as being separated from loved ones, meeting with enemies, not getting what we want and meeting with what we dislike. In the human realm, however, one does have the chance to practice the Dharma. When endowed with the eight freedoms and ten riches, the human body is the most perfect support for this practice.

Of the ten riches, five are from oneself: the circumstance of being born as a human, in a central country where the teachings are present, with one's senses intact, with faith in the teachings and having unperverted livelihood. The five riches from others are that a buddha has appeared, that he gave teachings, that the teachings remain, that people practice them and that one has found a teacher willing to accept one. When we possess all of these eighteen freedoms and riches we are said to have a precious human body which is like a wish-fulfilling jewel, and which is the unexcelled basis for Dharma practice.

Simply having a human body is not enough. As the text states, we also need faith. The four kinds of faith are admiration, strong interest, trusting faith, and unshakable confidence. Beginner's faith is called enthusiasm or admiration. As faith increases, it becomes longing or strong yearning. Finally it becomes full trust, which develops into unshakable confidence.

An example of the first type of faith is the happiness experienced if we go to a museum or temple, or if we come to a garden with beautiful flowers and think, "How nice! This is so pleasant." Whenever we find something which impresses or delights us and makes us happy, this is enthusiasm.

The example for longing faith is to have decided that we would like to attain for ourselves that which makes us happy, a material thing or some quality which we want to develop. In the spiritual sense, when we first meet a teacher we initially feel very impressed or inspired by him, enthusiastic. In the second stage we have decided that we wish to become like him ourselves. That is longing or yearning faith.

The third kind of faith is to feel trust in the teacher and in the spiritual qualities of his Body, Speech, and Mind. The fourth, an irreversible faith is unshakeable confidence, complete trust that arises only after the practitioner has attained some degree of realization of the awakened state of mind. Unless we are like Naropa, this type of faith is not easy to possess. If his master, Tilopa, said "Jump" he would jump; if Tilopa said "Die," Naropa would have done so. Without the confidence of realization such total trust does not genuinely happen.

The first two types of faith, admiration and longing, are easy to acquire but are also fickle and fluctuating. Trusting faith is eighty or ninety percent stable, but once in a while a slight doubt could be entertained, "If I jump, won't I die?" or "What is the purpose?"

Song of Karmapa

Irreversible faith transcends this questioning. We trust that our master is omniscient, a buddha in person, and that whatever he does in thought, word or deed is exclusively for the welfare of all beings and for promoting the Dharma. Although we may not understand his means, we don't get involved in questioning his purpose. The questioning attitude is necessary and in fact it is indispensable during the three earlier stages of faith, because at that stage we need to know what his intentions are.

We also need endeavor. This does not mean that once in a while we exert ourselves, trying to do something intensely. Correct endeavor is like the steady flow of a river or like a taut bowstring, neither too tight nor too loose. We need continual diligence, day by day, month by month, year by year. This does not occur suddenly. For countless aeons we have been bound by disturbing emotions and ignorance. As a result we have become accustomed to attachment, anger and stupidity, and this wrong habit prevents us from immediately clearing away these three poisons. We must be diligent. After a long period of diligence the qualities of virtue will increase, wisdom will unfold and we can attain that which was impossible before, enlightenment.

Finally, we need intelligence. Usually intelligence means the ability to discriminate and understand, but here it means being able to understand the teachings and apply them in practice. The Buddha himself said not to accept his teachings on face value alone, but to examine them as if you were buying gold. By testing it you will know whether or not the gold is of good quality, or whether it is even gold. Similarly, you should ascertain the meaning of the teachings through your own intelligence and study. Only by employing factual reasoning can you definitively decide. In that way, clear intelligence will unfold.

To follow an eminent spiritual guide means that among the many kinds of spiritual guides we should follow one with enlightened qualities. He should be unfailing and undeceiving. An excellent spiritual friend should be skilled in learning, reflection and meditation. His exposition of the teachings should be unhindered. He should be able to write freely, be able to compose teachings and he should be undefeatable in argument.

Through study, an eminent guide should have clarified any lack of understanding of the different teachings and practices. Having contemplated them, he should be free of doubt and misconception. Finally, as the result of meditation practice, the unerring wisdom should truly permeate his mind-stream. In short, the teacher should possess compassion, benevolence towards others and the wisdom that understands emptiness. He should have decided upon the view of Mahamudra free from constructs. Unerring realization gives rise to benevolence. Acting with benevolence, he will never lead us astray and never deceive us. He cannot possibly take us on a wrong path. He will only benefit beings and never act in an nondharmic way. Following such a teacher is called 'taking the support of an eminent guide.'

The teachings of our tradition state that the student should first be skilled in examining a spiritual guide, then in following him; and finally, in assimilating his realization. First, both teacher and student should examine each other. It is said that the student should examine the master for a long time to decide whether or not he is qualified. The teacher must examine the student as well. After they have done that and come to some agreement, then teachings can be given.

To simply follow a spiritual master and offer him nice meals, socialize and have conversations with him will not be of much help. You must receive some of his understanding. You may not be able to absorb all of his realization, but it is important to grasp the key points. Request the pure instructions and try to understand their meaning by clarifying all doubts. In short, first

Song of Karmapa

examine, then follow and finally receive the nectar of oral instructions. To receive the instructions and then give them up brings no benefit. Instead we should follow the example of Milarepa. He received Marpa's teachings, practiced them correctly and progressed through all the paths and levels in one lifetime.

We need to practice the instructions correctly, without being deterred by obstacles. There are outer, inner and secret obstacles. Outer obstacles are disturbances in the outer elements or in external conditions, such as attachment to food, clothing, reputation, dwelling place, family and so on, which distract us from practicing the Dharma. Inner obstacles, like feeling uncomfortable or sick, are disturbances in our channels and energies. An example of this is feeling restless or depressed and being unable to practice because of this. However, when we are involved in negative actions we usually feel alert and wide awake; this is a habitual pattern from past negative actions. Secret or innermost obstacles are when we give in to dullness or agitation while engaging in mediation training. Dualistic fixation also constitutes secret obstacles.

A profound correspondence exists between the external world and our physical body. Both are composite entities and therefore impermanent. The external world is composed of the five elements of earth, water, fire, wind and space, and our physical body is made of these same five elements. When they are in harmony we feel quite healthy and normal. However, when the five outer elements are out of balance, the objects of the outer world change shape or decompose. Likewise, a strong imbalance in the elements making up the human body heralds change, illness or death. For example, if the heat element predominates we feel thirsty, feverish or very uncomfortable. If the wind element becomes overpowering we feel hungry, nauseous or mentally confused. Whether or not one is a practitioner, an imbalance in the body's elements can result in a wide variety of illness and physical sensations.

An imbalance in the inner channels, energies and essences may cause us to feel disturbed during meditation, making us unable to concentrate. When practicing shamatha we cannot attain insight or move on to vipashyana practice. We might say, "I feel moody these days." For no apparent external reason our mind is disturbed, unsettled. These are the ways in which the inner and secret obstacles manifest.

Obstacles appear whenever we attempt something which is difficult yet meaningful. Complete enlightenment is the most worthwhile thing to achieve in life, but something always seems to prevent us from attaining buddhahood. These hindrances are our obscurations, the habits which lead us away from liberation. Being carried away by disturbing emotions is the basic hindrance.

Without falling under the power of obstacles, may we be able to practice the sacred teachings in all our lives, not merely in this one but in the next and all that follow.

By learning the scriptures and through reasoning we
    are freed from the veil of ignorance.
Through contemplating the oral instructions we
    overcome the darkness of doubt.
With the light resulting from meditation we illuminate
    the natural state as it is.
May the light of this threefold knowledge increase.

The three supports for realizing the ultimate view, the natural state as it is, are scriptures, reasoning and instructions. Scripture refers to the words of the Buddha and the statements of all the great panditas and accomplished masters. We can understand the teachings by relying on the Buddha's words, on the statements of enlightened masters, and also on our own reasoning.

Song of Karmapa

Learning gives rise to the first kind of knowledge, that which clears away the veil of not knowing what the teachings are or how to practice them. The second kind of knowledge is that which comes from contemplation. By thinking about the oral instructions we can clear away the darkness of doubts and misconceptions. The third kind of knowledge is the knowledge which results from meditation experience. With the light that comes from meditation we can illuminate the natural state as it is. May the light of this threefold knowledge increase, at first through understanding what we do not know, and later through expanding that understanding into deeper realization.

Again in reference to scriptures, oral instructions, and reasoning: Scriptures refer to that which the Buddha and great masters have said; oral instructions refer to the very short, concise and direct teachings which point out the nature of mind, such as the instructions of Mahamudra. Reasoning refers to logic, the use of our intelligence. The unmistaken quality of the scriptures, the unmistaken quality of the guru's oral instructions and the unmistaken quality of our own reasoning enable us to resolve the nature of things exactly: what is relative and what is absolute, what is superficial and what is real, how things seem to be and how they really are. Having resolved this, contemplate the oral instructions and your doubts will be cleared away. But that is not enough. It is through personal practice that we gain direct experience of the natural state as it really is.

The Buddha's teachings should be resolved through study, reflection, and meditation. Once we have resolved the teachings in these three ways, we begin to clear away defects such as ignorance, misunderstanding and doubt. We should not automatically accept something just because the Buddha has said it. Likewise, just because something was stated by the great masters of the past we should not blindly believe it. We must examine it with our own intelligence, asking "Is this really true?"

Song of Karmapa

Through these unmistaken qualities — of what the Buddha has said, of what the enlightened masters have stated, and of our own intelligence — we can obtain clear knowledge of things as they are.

Studying and reflecting can provide superficial knowledge, but not knowledge of things as they really are. To resolve this, the practice of meditation is essential. Learning and reflection will help in approaching the ultimate result, the state of complete enlightenment, but these alone are not sufficient. The knowledge resulting from meditation practice is the most vital. Even though human beings have arms and legs, the heart is the most vital part of the body. Likewise in order to attain enlightenment the knowledge resulting from meditation is the most vital. If you have plenty of time and are intelligent and industrious, then studying a lot is very good. Having studied and reflected, you can gain a clear understanding of the teachings. With a clear understanding of the stages of practice, it will be easy to apply them. You will know exactly what is the superficial and what is the actual truth and will be free from misunderstanding, ignorance and doubt. But if you lack the time or interest to engage in detailed study, then practice is the most important. It is possible to attain enlightenment through the practice of meditation with only a little study. On the other hand, merely studying and thinking about the teachings without practicing will not result in enlightenment.

In the past in Tibet, most people who studied, reflected and practiced were Sangha members, although lay men and women did as well. Someone without much time, interest, intelligence or diligence, can study only certain parts of the texts, practice them, and still attain enlightenment. The main point is not to fool yourself by focusing only on studies and thinking about the teachings. Begin to put them into practice and meditate.

When planning and conducting this life, most people seem to think only of how to use their time for aims that provide temporary comfort. People who are a little more interested in spiritual practice plan how to study and think about the Dharma. They use the major part of their lives learning the theory of the path to awakening and spend only a small part actually practicing. We should not fool ourselves in this way. No matter what we study, it is only words and concepts, not the ultimate truth itself. We can say 'this exists,' 'that does not exist,' 'this is empty' and 'that is not empty,' but all of these statements are only mental formulations, just conceptual thought. Any thought, good or bad, covers our true nature. Please understand this: use the greater part of your life for actual practice, not for studies or plans. The effect or result of practice is the realization of our nature, which is the unity of emptiness and compassion.

Through learning we clear away ignorance and through contemplation we clear away doubt, but we experience the natural state through meditation practice. It is said, "Do not rely on the expedient meaning, but on the true meaning. Do not rely on dualistic consciousness but on wisdom." Rely on the oral instructions to realize the natural state.

Questions and Answers

Student: I was thinking about how a student can utilize all the aspects which make up a precious human body. Maybe I was not listening properly, but I understood that one can have a human body with senses intact, be living in a good place where the Buddha's teachings are still present, have money and time but still not have the wish to practice. That seems to be the ultimate factor; without that wish you can have all the other conditions but they will not lead to Dharma practice. Is that correct?

Rinpoche: To have a good house you need the foundation, walls, roof and pillars; having only one of these is not enough. Likewise, to practice we need all of the eight freedoms and the ten riches. One of these riches is to have 'faith in the right place', in Buddhism, as Tibetans have had for centuries. In Tibet there have been many masters and there are still many masters people can meet. Few Tibetans lack faith in the Buddha, Dharma and Sangha. Only a very few do not believe in the cause and effect of actions. Tibetans usually go to monasteries and light butter lamps, visit lamas, give donations and receive blessing cords, but they leave it at that. Therefore, very few of them attain liberation. This is not because their actions are pointless. Through these actions some negative karmas are purified, some merit is accumulated. But attaining liberation through simply having faith would take too long. More than superficial faith is required.

Student: This question concerns the streams of virtue undefiled by the threefold concepts. What difference does it make if water is defiled or not?

Rinpoche: When an action is embraced by our understanding of emptiness, it is automatically free from the threefold concepts and is therefore undefiled like clear water. If our actions are not embraced by emptiness they are like defiled water. Someone who is about to die of thirst in a desert would drink dirty, disgusting water rather than die. Compared to being without any water, defiled water is quite good; it can quench our thirst. But if we live in a place with good water we would of course prefer to drink clean, pure water, the special mineral water. Thus we say that virtue embraced by the view of emptiness is the perfect virtue, undefiled like pure, natural water.

Student: What qualities should a qualified Vajrayana student possess? And how does one assimilate the teacher's realization?

Song of Karmapa

Rinpoche: First, the student should be as stable as a mountain. Here 'stable' means not just to run after any spiritual teacher, but after examining the teacher to see whether he is good or not, to be consistent in following him. In other words, in your thoughts and deeds keep complete trust in the teachings, in the teacher's actions and in what he represents. A good Vajrayana practitioner should be stable in his relations with Dharma friends and in his respect towards the teacher. There is no stability in having faith one day and not the next. Try to be stable like a mountain. This means being patient and not short-tempered. Just as a master should not be short-tempered with the student, if the master says something which we do not like or understand, we should not immediately become angry and lose faith. We should try to be open to the possibility that there might be some point to his comment. With our present level of realization, it is quite unlikely that we will always understand the teacher's intentions. So we should be patient and not short-tempered.

The student should also be flexible like gold. Gold can be hammered, melted and transformed into different shapes and ornaments. It is very pliable. An open-minded student can digest whatever instructions the teacher gives about how to change his character, and he can apply them to improve himself. If one is rigid like iron, it is difficult to change.

The third quality a student needs is vast learning, which should be all-encompassing as the ocean. We should seek to study and understand the Dharma teachings in a very vast way. Our minds should be clear and transparent like the ocean. We should be free from doubt and uncertainty. We should be well-versed in the topics of knowledge and be able to encompass the more profound Dharma teachings.

Diligence is the fourth quality. One's diligence should be like the steady flow of a river; not sometimes striving and sometimes slack, but always steadfast.

Song of Karmapa

Someone possessing these four qualities is a qualified student. The worst student is the one who begins with a lot of enthusiasm, but who becomes less and less interested and more and more lazy as time goes by. The better student starts slowly with a small amount of practice and then gradually increases it.

Now to answer the second part of your question on how to assimilate the master's realization. This assimilation depends, as mentioned earlier, on the master being qualified and the student possessing these four qualities. The main point is that the student should not adhere too closely to the words of the teaching, but rather to their intended meaning. The student should try to apply the meaning to his own personal experience. When one is completely clear about the inner nature of the teaching and when misunderstandings and doubts are cleared away, then one's realization and the master's realization will be identical, beyond increase and decrease.

Student: What about the relationship between student and teacher?

Rinpoche: Tantric teachings instruct that one should keep pure perception or 'sacred outlook' towards one's teacher, and that someone who regards his teacher as a buddha in person receives great blessings. This does not mean that he is *the* Buddha — he is still one's teacher, of course. But if you regard the teacher as just an ordinary person, the blessings will be much less. The important thing is that understanding takes place through the openness that results from the power of trust and confidence. It is best to regard one's teacher as a true buddha. If one cannot regard him as that, then one should at least regard him as a genuine bodhisattva. Thinking of him as only an ordinary person makes it more difficult to receive the blessings.

Student: What are the powers which the Buddha called the inconceivable power of material substance, the

Song of Karmapa

inconceivable power of mantric sound and the inconceivable power of samadhi or concentration?

Rinpoche: These powers have degrees of strength. The power of mantra is stronger than that of substance and the power of samadhi is stronger than that of mantra. The power of samadhi, emphasized during the Buddha's time, is the way in which 80,000 practitioners could simultaneously display miraculous actions through their power of concentration, such as flying from one mountaintop to another. The power of mantric sound is illustrated by different kinds of magic. Whether black or white magic, certain spells or incantations can change people's attitudes and overcome their aversions; in some cases magic even kills.

Finally there is the power of substance which can be illustrated by the power that is released by splitting an atom. Why then don't people with the power of samadhi use this to subdue nuclear power? We must consider the difference between individual karma and the general karma of sentient beings, and also remember that this age is characterized as the time of the five degenerations. The degeneration of material substances is that material substances are used in ways which bring no benefit. The five degenerations of this age are part of the general karma shared by all beings, while our individual pleasures and pains belong to each particular person's karma.

The Buddha's main work was simply teaching people the Dharma. "I am showing you the path," he said. "Whether or not you traverse it is up to yourself. Enlightenment lies in your own hand: do not think that you will be sent to the pure realms as easily as throwing a stone." The Buddha also said, "The karma of sentient beings is not something I can cleanse as easily as rinsing with water. It is not possible to throw all sentient beings into the state of enlightenment."

Student: If we are to overcome doubt by questioning and reasoning, how can we accept a seemingly incorrect view such as the Buddha's teachings about geography?

Rinpoche: Whether or not we are Buddhist, it might seem strange that such an intelligent person as Buddha Shakyamuni said that the world was flat with four continents and a huge mountain in the middle. Some people may say, "I cannot trust in teachings like that, they do not make any sense." But there is no real conflict. The Buddha taught with skillful means and compassion and the people to whom he taught were accustomed to a certain world view. So he taught the two levels of truth.

Relative, conventional truth can be seen to be whatever anyone understands or perceives. An old field worker who has not studied philosophy simply sees earth as earth and stones as stones without many ideas beyond that. He may not have the capacity or the scope to see beyond relative truth. The Buddha accepted conventional truth, though he saw beyond it. Had the Buddha spoken in those days of a big iron contraption with wheels that moved on thousands of miles of track, seating hundreds of people at once and travelling from one place to another, nobody would have believed anything he said. It would have sounded like complete nonsense. But these days nobody is amazed to hear about people traveling in railroad trains.

Likewise, during the Buddha's time the most prevalent world view was that of the Hindu Vedas, which described the four continents and Mount Sumeru. Buddha simply adopted this, so his teachings did not conflict with the existing world view. This was done through skillful means and compassion.

Nowadays we have a different world view. Because we can fly around the world in any direction and arrive back in the same place, we therefore deduce that the world is round. With telescopes we can even see other worlds. We may someday see beings living on other worlds who fly around in flat things that do not seem to run on gasoline as our cars do. The Buddha actually taught that the world system which we inhabit is not the only human world. He taught that there are one billion other worlds in our part of the universe called a world system. Moreover, this is not the only world system; countless others exist. What scientists are now discovering is coming close to what the Buddha said a long time ago. We need not see any conflict there.

The Abhidharma teaches that first the world is formed and that after some time it finally disintegrates. The Tibetan word for world translates literally as 'support for destruction.' It is taught that at the end of this aeon the world will be destroyed by seven suns, then water, and finally wind. In this era of nuclear weapons we can understand this. If all existing nuclear weapons were exploded simultaneously the world would probably blow apart. This is not impossible. The Buddha explained that at the end of a certain period of time seven suns will blow up the world and that it will then be washed away by water and finally scattered by wind so that nothing remains. We need not take this literally.

2

THE UNMISTAKEN WAY

*Through the nature of the ground, the two truths free
   from the extremes of eternalism and nihilism,
And the supreme path, the two accumulations free from
   the limits of exaggeration and denigration,
We attain the fruition of the two benefits free from the
   extremes of existence and peace.
May we connect with such a teaching free from error.*

This verse explains the view of Mahamudra. Rangjung Dorje taught that the nature of the ground is the two truths free from the extremes of eternalism and nihilism. If we fall into the extreme of eternalism, thinking that there is something permanent, or into the extreme of nihilism, thinking that there is nothing, we do not possess the correct view. To hold onto something as concrete is to be as foolish as a cow, but to hold onto nothingness is even more foolish. The right view is free from the two extremes of eternalism and nihilism.

Nagarjuna described these two wrong views, saying that the view of eternalism, the idea of holding on to a self as being as concrete and solid as Mount Sumeru, is not as bad as the nihilistic view that everything is totally void. The vital point is to arrive at the correct view that transcends both these extremes.

Song of Karmapa

The unity of the two truths is the ground of what should be realized. The relative truth is said to be true on the level of our experience, whereas the ultimate truth is true on the level of the essence which is our own nature. This means that whatever appears to sentient beings, whatever they experience, is true as relative truth. Whatever is experienced by a practitioner who has realization of his nature, is true as ultimate truth.

Nagarjuna taught that the six kinds of sentient beings have different ways of experiencing the same thing. Although in comparison to higher beings, the experiences of lower beings are less valid, they still consider their particular experience to be true. For example, a hell-being perceives water as molten metal, whereas a hungry ghost perceives it as pus and rotten blood and animals as something to drink. Human beings perceive it as water: thus, our perception is more real than that of lower beings. However, the gods' perception of water as nectar is even more real, and compared even to that, someone with realization of emptiness will perceive water just as it is. These different views result from varying levels and degrees of obscuration, which, as they are cleared away, allow one to come closer to seeing things as they really are.

Relative truth is things as they appear; ultimate truth is things as they are, their essential nature. Every thing in the world and all the beings contained in it represent relative truth in the sense of being dependent upon one another. Everything with characteristics depends upon something else. For example, left exists because there is right. The same for up and down, mother and child; one is defined dependent upon the other. Everything appears due to the interdependence of causes and conditions, and is all called relative or conventional truth. This illusory display is how things appear, relatively. Ultimate truth, on the other hand, is the very nature of things free from any characteristics. The ultimate truth of all inanimate and animate objects is beyond characteristics, just as space is devoid of any constructs whatsoever. It is beyond description, thought and words, and surpasses the reach of the intellect. It has never been liberated or confused, nor has it known existence or nonexistence. This state is called the primordial lord, the ultimate state of Mahamudra.

The two truths cannot be separated; they are a unity. All things, all the phenomena of samsara and nirvana, appear and can be experienced, but if closely examined they do not possess any true existence. They appear but have no self-nature. No matter how appearance is examined, whether through scriptural statements or logic, the conclusion we come to is that appearance is illusion, like a dream possessing no true existence. Under examination phenomena seem to appear like a reflection in a mirror — completely devoid of mental constructs or extremes, devoid of true existence. Understanding this, simultaneously clears away the extremes of both eternalism and nihilism. We should understand that all things, all phenomena, while being empty, still appear as unceasing manifestation. Everything can take place, there is a potential for everything to unfold. Understanding that destroys the view of nihilism. In short, the ground is the unity of the two truths free from the extremes of eternalism and nihilism.

The supreme path is the two accumulations of merit and wisdom, free from the limits of exaggeration and denigration. Exaggeration is saying "there is something" and denigration is saying "there is nothing." Through the ground and the path we attain the fruition of the two benefits: benefit for ourselves and benefit for others. This fruition is free from the extremes of existence and peace, samsara and nirvana. Practicing without the unity of means and knowledge will cause us to fall into either the extreme of existence, which is samsara, or the extreme of the peace of nirvana. Therefore we must possess the unity of means and knowledge. Thus, may we connect with such a teaching free from error, free from any mistakes or distractions.

The ground of purification is mind essence, the union of being empty and cognizant.
That which purifies is the great vajra-like practice of Mahamudra.
May we realize the immaculate dharmakaya — the fruition of having purified
All the passing stains of confusion, that are to be purified.

Four aspects are mentioned here. The first line refers to the basis, the ground for purification; the second to the method of purification; the third to fruition which is the result of purification; and the fourth line describes what is actually cleared away — the passing stains of confusion.

The phrase 'ground of purification' points to our basic nature. It refers to the view of Mahamudra which is described as being free from mental fabrications or thought constructs, as well as all notions of extremes.

To obtain complete liberation and unhindered omniscience, we must first clear away the various obstacles which are our obscurations. In order to do that we must be able to identify the ground for purification — the nature of our mind. What characterizes the nature of mind? Its essence is empty and its nature cognizant. It is not limited to being just empty or just cognizant; these two are a natural unity, like water being naturally wet or fire naturally hot.

We must resolve this natural state for ourselves, through personal experience. We can approach the mind's undivided emptiness and cognizance either by studying scriptures; through the unmistaken quality of the Buddha's own words and the statements of noble beings, masters and panditas of the past; or by way of our own powers of reason. Utilizing these three, we should determine how the natural state of mind actually is. For example, in the *Prajnaparamita*, the Enlightened One said: "Mind is not the dualistic mind. It is the cognizant nature." The mind is empty and cognizant, as a unity. *The Uttara Tantra* says: "The nature of mind is luminous." It is like space, unchanging and perfectly pure. The stains of attachment, anger, and stupidity are like clouds that temporarily cover the sky, they are passing: not inherent.

We hold that we are conscious and that we have a mind, yet this 'mind' is impossible to find as a concrete object with color and shape. On the other hand we can hardly say that mind is nothingness, void nonexistence like space, because it thinks of different things and experiences different emotions. Anything at all can occur in the mind. Thus, it is said to be both empty and cognizant.

Only by remaining in equanimity can we resolve uncertainty about the natural, unerring state of mind and purify our disturbing emotions. Otherwise the basis for our understanding is intellectual and dependent on words, without real benefit. Some people may think the mind is a conscious entity, while others believe it is utterly empty. One hears people say, "The clarity is like the light of the sun, the emptiness is like space." To understand this in a literal way and cling to it, is detrimental for resolving the correct view.

Mind essence is sometimes called buddha nature, tathagatagarbha. It has several other names, but regardless of what we call it, unless we realize our own nature and acknowledge its simplicity, we continuously stray into samsaric existence. Bound by confusion, conceptual thinking and disturbing emotions, we roam through the three realms, one after the other. Again and again we find ourselves among the six classes of sentient beings. This results from grasping at appearances. How are the three realms characterized? They are the nature of suffering and the expanse of delusion. This is not ultimate truth, but the way it appears. If we study, reflect, and meditate, gradually we will understand this view and be able to purify our obscurations.

"That which purifies is the great vajra-like practice of Mahamudra." What has to be purified are temporary delusions, confusion, karma and disturbing emotions. There are many details to consider here such as the 84,000 disturbing emotions. The most profound, quick and supreme method for purification is that which is taught in this *Song of Mahamudra.*

In order to realize the nature of mind, we must first meet a qualified teacher. We need to follow someone who is competent and who perceives the innate truth. When the student who has become a suitable vessel meets a true master, the student must request the pith instructions for practice.

The general system of practice begins with the common and special preliminaries. The general preliminaries are the 'Four Mind Changings' which turn one's mind from samsaric pursuits. These are recognizing the difficulty of obtaining a precious human body, realizing the fact of impermanence and death, accepting the law of karma and acknowledging the defects of samsara. Reflect on these well; they are not difficult to understand. Do not merely acknowledge them, they must truly be taken to heart. Do that and you will become the best Dharma practitioner; otherwise you will merely be a mediocre practitioner. Without a deep understanding of these four mind changings, we will never accept samsara as pointless. Without becoming completely weary with samsara, we cannot genuinely be interested in achieving liberation. Our Dharma practice will then be a long, long path.

Later we undertake the special preliminaries which are special methods for purifying the obscurations of our body, speech and mind as well as the combination of these three. These are called the 'preliminaries of the four or five times one hundred thousand' and they have been taught out of skillful means and great compassion.

Song of Karmapa

They include recitation of the refuge and bodhisattva vows along with prostrations, Vajrasattva recitation, mandala offering and guru yoga.

Engaging in the preliminaries prepares us for receiving the various Vajrayana transmissions; the elaborate, unelaborate, very unelaborate and extremely unelaborate empowerments. When the vajra master bestows these empowerments, there are two aspects: the words and the meaning. Although many teachers give empowerments these days and many people attend them, one needs certainty regarding the view of the ground to really experience the meaning and not just the words of an empowerment. Furthermore, a disciple should see the teacher as a Buddha in person and have faith, confidence and trust in him in order to receive the empowerment.

These four empowerments, also called the vase empowerment, secret empowerment, wisdom-knowledge empowerment and precious word empowerment, are indispensable for Vajrayana practice. The very profound practices connected with each of these four empowerments enable us to attain complete enlightenment within this very lifetime. However, and this cannot be emphasized enough, these practices cannot be taught to just anyone. Unless a person has openness and faith in the Buddha's teachings, the empowerments will not be of much benefit.

Of the four empowerments, the vase empowerment is usually given with the master seated on a throne, the shrine beautifully arranged and decorated and with the disciples sitting on lower seats making mandala offerings. At that moment they feel great interest and devotion. The master then reveals the mandala and confers the empowerment by placing a vase and other ritual implements on the top of each person's head. Later he explains the ritual to them. That is the general procedure in a vase empowerment.

Song of Karmapa

The nature of empowerment does not depend upon external circumstances such as the precise laying out and utilizing of ritual implements made of precious metals. The actual conferring of the empowerment depends upon the karmic readiness of the student and the wisdom and blessings of the master. The great Indian master Maitripa found his root guru, Shavaripa, only after undergoing great hardships as he travelled around in search of a master. When he finally found Shavaripa, he was overjoyed, believing that he finally had the opportunity to formally request the vase empowerment. But Shavaripa merely placed his hands upon Maitripa's head. In that very instant, due to the auspicious coincidence of a qualified master meeting with a qualified student, Maitripa was introduced to and recognized the nature of the vase empowerment. In this case the empowerment was conferred very simply. Stories about Naropa, Milarepa and other great masters tell more about the various styles of empowerment.

One such story is about a Tibetan man named Khyungpo Naljor, the Garuda Yogi, who was the main disciple of Niguma, the great Indian yogini. Khyungpo Naljor had great faith in his teacher, Niguma. When the time came for conferring empowerment, Niguma filled a skull cup with excrement mixed into it instead of the usual sacred substances and asked Khyungpo Naljor to drink. Since he had one-pointed devotion and a mind free from any suspicion or doubt, Khyungpo Naljor drank the mixture and instantly recognized the nature of the empowerment.

The vase empowerment is the authorization to practice the development stage, to visualize the deity and to experience its vivid presence and the purity of the surrounding environment. When one actually perceives all phenomena as the unity of appearance and emptiness, one is said to have truly received the vase empowerment. In short, recognizing the wakefulness in which appearance and emptiness are inseparable is called the vase empowerment. One recognizes one's physical body, composed of the elements and aggregates, as being divine in nature, empty and yet visible. Recognizing this plants the seed or cause for the realization of nirmanakaya.

The secret empowerment refers to understanding the key points of the energy-winds and the practices connected with them such as tummo, through which one realizes the unity of luminosity and emptiness. By recognizing this the seed for attaining sambhogakaya is planted. This is called obtaining the secret empowerment.

Next is the wisdom-knowledge empowerment. Stories are told of great masters from the past such as Naropa, Tilopa and Saraha, who attained high degrees of realization through the practices connected to this empowerment. However, the person who engages in the practices related to the third empowerment must already possess the correct view; otherwise he or she is no different from an ordinary worldly person. For example, Saraha was the most disciplined of the five hundred monks in his monastery, but he later took an arrow maker's daughter as his consort. After practicing with her for some time he said, "Before, I was not a pure monk, but now I am," which is quite an outrageous statement for a monk who had taken a wife. But he declared, "If I am still a pure monk, may the River Ganges be my witness and flow backwards." The river did indeed flow backwards, proving that he remained a genuine monk.

Through the fourth empowerment, the word empowerment, all of samsara and nirvana is resolved to be equal in nature. One realizes the state of unity beyond concepts, planting the seed for realizing the svabhavikakaya, the essence body which is the last of the four kayas. The fourth empowerment means that the master points out coemergent wisdom and the student realizes it as it is. This state of innate wakefulness is the

Song of Karmapa

absence of mental fabrication, and is also known as ordinary mind, fresh and unmodified.

When the perfect conditions of a suitable disciple and a qualified master come together, and the disciple requests and receives the pith instructions and understands them, then he or she is introduced to the wisdom of realization. These days, many masters frequently give a variety of empowerments and disciples flock to participate in these ceremonies. To receive an empowerment in its deepest sense, however, one must understand the correct view.

The Kagyüpas speak of this correct view as being ordinary mind, inherent wisdom, thatness and the unfabricated Mahamudra. One should be introduced to the genuine! There are different methods of giving the pointing-out instructions: pointing-out by word, symbol, sign or simply by resting in meditative composure. This can happen when a qualified master and a suitable disciple meet. It has happened many times in the past and is definitely possible in the present.

In order to sustain the view, the practitioner of Mahamudra should first recognize buddha nature, then train in it, and finally attain stability. In order to recognize buddha nature, we must identify exactly what is preventing us from realizing it now and what needs to be cleared away — all the passing stains of confusion. Where did these passing stains come from? The ground itself, the buddha nature, is without impurity or confusion, but the temporary defilements, the stains of confusion, result from not having recognized the state of the ground.

What is the fruition? The immaculate dharmakaya is the fruition of having purified these stains. Through practice, we unveil a state free from all dualistic phenomena, free from holding onto subject and object, perceiver and perceived. Having totally discarded all the different ways of being mistaken, having rid oneself of the passing stains, we realize dharmakaya, the ground itself exactly as it is. This is the fruition of purification.

The moment we realize the dharmakaya, the two other kayas are spontaneously attained, even though the song does not make this explicit. Dharmakaya itself is beyond any mental constructs. Sambhogakaya is endowed with the thirty-two major and eighty minor marks of excellence as well as with the five perfections: the perfection of the teacher, retinue, teaching, time and place. On the level of sambhogakaya, the teacher is always the perfectly enlightened Buddha, the retinue always consists of bodhisattvas dwelling on the bodhisattva levels. The nirmanakaya manifests in different ways in order to help beings. Some nirmanakaya beings display a beautiful form and some an ugly one, while some are not particularly notable. They act in accordance with the needs of sentient beings. For example, a single buddha can display a billion different bodies and appear in a billion different worlds simultaneously. Some nirmanakayas are like Buddha Shakyamuni who, through the twelve deeds, accomplished various achievements such as turning the wheel of Dharma and so forth. Although our text only mentions the dharmakaya, the rupakaya, meaning the sambhogakaya and the nirmanakaya, are automatically implied.

To have cut misconceptions of the ground is the confidence of the view.
To sustain that undistractedly is the key point of meditation.
To train in all the points of practice is the supreme action.
May we possess the confidence of view, meditation and action.

To be without any misconceptions of the ground is to possess the confidence of the view. The basic view of Mahamudra is free from all kinds of mental constructs. The ground wisdom, which is the basic wakefulness or nature of the mind, is empty yet cognizant, empty while *being* cognizant. These two aspects are in fact indivisible. As Mipham Rinpoche said, "The nature of things is primordially pure and therefore defies the extreme of existence. Since its cognizant nature is spontaneously present it also excludes the extreme of nonexistence." Thus the nature of mind, our enlightened essence, is the unity of emptiness and cognizance. To recognize this is the essential point of the view.

In this context 'cognizant' means knowing without fixating on what is perceived. While the essence of this perception is empty, there remains a clarity totally devoid of conceptualization, a cognizance free from holding onto anything. This is the Mahamudra of cognizant emptiness. Simply rest in a natural state which is empty but at the same time vividly awake, cognizant and free from fixation; this is the essence of Mahamudra.

Mahamudra means to look directly while resting free from fabrication. 'Looking' is only a word we use. There is really no concrete thing looked at or into, no one who looks and no real act of looking. Although cognizance is devoid of these three concepts, we must use some word to approximate the true meaning, so we use the word 'look'.

The view of Mahamudra is also called 'ordinary mind,' which refers to the wisdom dwelling within, innate wakefulness. As long as our mind is obscured by and occupied with mundane thoughts which are the usual concepts involving the five poisons and dualistic fixations, then the ordinary mind of innate wakefulness is covered up. Yet the moment normal thoughts and fixations are absent, the ordinary mind, ground wisdom, is immediately and vividly present. 'Ordinary' as used in 'ordinary mind' means not fabricated, altered or changed by any thought constructs. As soon as a deluded thought is fabricated in the mind then that state of mind is no longer ordinary; it is artificial. Ordinary mind means simply resting in naturalness.

Song of Karmapa

The word Mahamudra literally means 'great seal,' indicating that all the phenomena of samsara and nirvana as well as of the path are included within the state of indivisible compassion and emptiness. These phenomena appear nowhere other than within the "seal," or the reach, of empty and compassionate mind. Thus it is called *mudra* or seal. It is *maha*, or great, because it is the highest or greatest method of conquering the disturbing emotions.

Various misconceptions can arise concerning the view. We may become sidetracked, misinterpret the teachings, or acquire a totally distorted version of what is meant by 'view.' We may attach some meaning to the natural state which it does not possess. Do not grasp at the words while abandoning the meaning. Some people understand the meaning but are ignorant of the words and are therefore unable to teach. Others may be skilled in words but ignorant of the meaning, never having really experienced it. We must be free from both kinds of ignorance. Sometimes we formulate an imaginary version of how the natural state must be and then cling to this representation as truly being 'it.' This is simply another conceptual creation which is mistaken and deluded. To experience the natural state as it truly is, we must cut through our intellectual ideas of how we think it is. We must gain confidence in the correct view.

We must experience the ground, the natural state which is the view of Mahamudra. To attain confidence in this view we must cut misconceptions by means of our own understanding, experience, and finally realization. But, having the confidence of the view is not enough: we must implement our realization. Once we recognize the correct view, we may feel assured of our ability to really understand the nature of mind, but this in itself is insufficient. The key point of meditation is that the view be sustained without distraction, and at best this means continuously, throughout both day and night. This is very difficult.

Song of Karmapa

Usually we set a time each day to sit down on our cushion and engage in meditation practice. During most of the rest of the day we are carried away by distractions, caught up in thoughts about preparing good food, acquiring new clothes, enhancing our homes or improving our reputations. To some extent we may believe that these things are important. But realize that countless hours are lost due to laziness and pursuance of the five sense objects.

There is a Tibetan saying: "The mind is fickle and appearances are beguiling." We are like children whose heads are easy to turn. Children can immediately switch moods. In the middle of a meal a child will suddenly feel an urge to run outside and play. Likewise, to bodhisattvas and buddhas, we seem like spoiled children with bad habits; our present state of mind is quite childish. Once we have recognized the view of Mahamudra we should try to sustain it undistractedly. However, there are many outer and inner distractions, and in addition to being easily distracted we are also quite lazy. The crucial point of meditation practice is to maintain the view without distraction.

To sum up: the essence of meditation is recognition of the view. Having been introduced to the true view of Mahamudra, the practitioner with confidence in the view should maintain it continually and undistractedly. The practice is to first recognize, then to train and then to attain stability in that recognition. The supreme action is training in maintaining the view undistractedly.

The Mahamudra system uses the Six Doctrines of Naropa as an enhancement practice. Other enhancement practices are development and completion stages, but the ultimate enhancement practice is to maintain the view undistractedly. Have the aspiration to possess the confidence of the perfect view, the perfect meditation, and the perfect action.

This view, shared by Mahamudra, Madhyamika and Dzogchen, is transcendent knowledge beyond words, thoughts and description. The action is not to separate oneself from the view and meditation. If you possess such a view, meditation and action, you cannot avoid attaining the fruition of dharmakaya, ordinary mind. The meditation that is empty in essence yet cognizant in nature is to be undistractedly maintained. Have confidence in the view, meditation, and action, and you will achieve the ultimate fruition, the realization of buddhahood. That is what we aspire towards.

All phenomena are the illusory display of mind.
Mind is devoid of 'mind' — empty of any entity.
Empty and yet unceasing, it manifests as anything whatsoever.
Realizing this completely, may we cut its basis and root.

When we have realized the correct view of Mahamudra devoid of any mental fabrication, we are totally free from the defects of partial understanding, misunderstanding or doubt. Therefore we naturally resolve all phenomena as the illusory display of mind.

Understanding all phenomena to be the mind's illusory display, how do we resolve the nature of the mind itself? The view is that the essence of mind is empty. What we usually call 'mind' is that which thinks, feels and conceives all different kinds of ideas about everything. In the second line, devoid of mind means that mind is without concreteness; no shape, color or material substance can be found. Saying that the essence of mind is empty means that it cannot be established as existent. However, it is not blank nothingness like space. While empty in essence, it still manifests unceasingly and unobstructedly in multifarious ways. When we examine the natural state closely through learning, contemplating and meditating, we can clear away all doubts and misconceptions about this. To cut its basis and root means to arrive at such certainty.

Song of Karmapa

Questions and Answers

Student: What does 'to be deluded' mean?

Rinpoche: It means to be mistaken. Are we mistaken or deluded about anything? What does it mean to be deluded? What does it mean to be without delusion? What is it that we call 'confusion' or 'delusion?' If we first study and then really contemplate these questions we will be able to cut the basic root of ignorance or delusion.

Where does realization of nonconceptual wakefulness come from? The basic state of the ground is completely free from any thought constructs, so why is it not realized? We have been unable to realize it because it is obscured by ignorance and disturbing emotions.

We can ask "Does space exist or not?" We have to say that space exists because it accommodates the world. The universe is formed, disintegrates and reforms in space. Space functions in that it makes a place for things to appear and occur. Therefore we must say that it exists. But where is space? What is it like? Can you point to it? It has no form, color or location. The natural state of mind is like space. Just as space can be obscured by clouds, the ground nature can be obscured by dualistic thinking and confusion.

The space which is obscured by clouds is not the real space; it is space which is covered by some 'stains.' Although space itself is not changed or tainted by clouds, it is still obscured. Applying that analogy to the mind, we can see how delusion covers the natural state, hindering us from seeing clearly.

Student: What are the two obscurations?

Rinpoche: The two obscurations are the obscuration of disturbing emotions and the obscuration of dualistic knowledge. Disturbing emotions are the three mind poisons. The obscuration of dualistic knowledge is misunderstanding the nature of reality in conjunction with discursive thought. This second obscuration is sometimes divided into two, the so-called third obscuration being habitual tendencies, the potential for negative emotions to arise even though they are not actively present. For instance if we have a bottle which once contained whisky, a trace of the whisky odor will still linger even after it is thoroughly rinsed with soap and water. This tendency to linger occurs with habitual patterns as well.

To purify the two obscurations and thereby obtain the two kayas, we need to gather the two accumulations: the accumulation of merit with a focus and the accumulation of wisdom beyond focus. Doing prostrations or circumambulating or thinking of the Three Jewels accumulates merit with a focal point. Thinking "I have negative karma which must be purified" and forming the aspiration "May all my negative actions be purified," and then reciting a few mantras is beneficial skillful means. A more skilled aspect to this, however, is to really understand emptiness. A moment of seeing emptiness is very profound, a great accumulation of merit without a focal or reference point. The practitioner who understands emptiness accumulates a tremendous amount of merit.

Student: What can a disciple do in order to realize the true meaning of empowerment?

Rinpoche: There are different types of readiness. The karmic result of a person who possesses the effect of former training, who has practiced in the past or in a past life, is that at the time of the empowerment he or she may be just at the point of recognizing mind nature. For example, a child may not have seen his mother for many years, but when he suddenly meets her again the recognition is immediate. However, a child who has never seen his mother would find it more difficult to recognize her. Likewise, the person who has already practiced is more ready to recognize what is transmitted as the nature of empowerment.

What kind of practices will make us more ready? The Kagyü tradition teaches that having faith and devotion while keeping pure samaya facilitates the realization. In general, we must accumulate merit and avoid negative actions. This is like building a staircase enabling us to reach the roof of a house; the staircase has no use except to take us to the roof. This is why training and practice are very important. The teachings say, "When karmic misdeeds are purified, realization occurs spontaneously." That is the whole logic behind purification.

Student: If a practitioner associates with samaya breakers and demonic types of people, does that increase obscurations? And if so, what is the most immediate method for purification of that obscuration?

Rinpoche: Vajrayana practice involves the creation of samaya. There are many details, but in essence samaya refers to the relationship between the student, the teacher, and the teaching. The most important point in Vajrayana practice is the teaching that enables one to recognize and realize the nature of mind, the basic wakefulness. The teacher who shows the student how to clearly recognize this, who points it out, is traditionally called one's 'root guru.' People who practice together, who have recognized their mind essence and share these teachings, are called vajra friends. A violation of this samaya bond occurs when vajra friends fight, experience disharmony or hold wrong views about each other or their teacher. Since they are bound through a shared samaya, disrupting the harmony, breaks this bond.

The teachings say that associating with people who have turned against the mandala, against the community, is like a mirror becoming obscured by vapors. If you breathe on the surface of a mirror, suddenly you cannot see much anymore. When influenced by this obscuration, the mind is disturbed and progress slows down. Associating with samaya violators causes one's ability to meditate to diminish, along with one's devotion and compassion. Studying, contemplating and practicing the teachings become more difficult. At best one should not associate with such people; at least one should not be influenced by them. If one feels that someone else has broken samaya, one should not hate him but generate compassion. Should one's 'mirror' become a little clouded, the best method by which to resolve the problem is Vajrasattva recitation and meditation. Vajrasattva practice and compassion are the two most important remedies.

3

NO CONTRADICTIONS

We have mistaken our nonexistent personal experience to be the objects,
And by the power of ignorance, mistaken self-cognizance to be a 'self.'
This dualistic fixation has made us wander in the sphere of samsaric existence.
May we cut ignorance and confusion at the very root.

In the first line, 'nonexistent' means that there is not a single outer object which can be proven to be permanent, real or substantially existent. All phenomena simply seem to appear through interdependence, which gives everything the nature of being like a dream or a magical illusion.

All dependent phenomena, the existence of which is defined by and therefore dependent upon other dependent phenomena, reveal their total lack of true existence the very moment they are placed under close scrutiny. There is not even a hair-tip of true existence to be found. Thus, 'nonexistent' means that all phenomena in themselves, from the very outset, do not possess any 'thing' that one can establish as being either permanent or real. Yet they do exist in our personal experience, to the same extent as a hallucination exists for the person under the influence of drugs. By the power of our deluded notion of things existing as independent entitics, combined with our disturbing emotions, we are tied up in dualistic fixation and mistakenly perceive things in terms of subject and object.

By the power of ignorance we have mistaken self-cognizance to be a 'self.' Our self-cognizance is truly a self-cognizant wakefulness, but because of confusion we take this to be a concrete 'I' or self. The third line means that for the six kinds of beings the basis of samsaric existence in the three realms is caused by ignorance, which is the first of the twelve links of interdependence. Ignorance leads to karmic formations and then to cognition. One after another the rest of the twelve links unfold, through name and form, the six sense bases, contact, sensation, grasping, craving, becoming, birth, old age and death. This continues on and on, one creating the cause for the next. One follows after the other like the pots on the rim of a water wheel.

Not knowing the natural state, the nature of our minds, we have been circling in samsara in the past and will continue to do so in the future. Therefore we make the aspiration, "May we cut ignorance and confusion at its very root." May we become totally clear about and resolve exactly what this ignorance and confusion is. Despite our nature, which is self-aware wisdom, through the power of ignorance and ego-clinging we have become deluded. Thus we have fallen under and grown accustomed to the power of dualistic fixation, causing us to wander aimlessly in samsaric existence.

The cause or seed of this deep-rooted delusion is ignorance. Ignorance is delusion, awareness is nondelusion. We should become very clear about the nature of this delusion, exerting ourselves in the means for clearing it away.

Song of Karmapa

It is not existent since even the victorious ones do not see it.
It is not nonexistent since it is the basis of samsara and nirvana.
This is not a contradiction but the Middle Way of unity.
May we realize the nature of mind, free from extremes.

This verse points out the view of the Middle Way, Madhyamika, which is free from the extremes of existence and nonexistence. It is the correct and most eminent view. The Dzogchen teachings illustrate this by stating that because dharmakaya is primordial purity, the extreme of permanence is cleared away, while because the manifestation of awareness is spontaneously present, the extreme of nihilism is eliminated.

What this actually means is that the nature of mind is not something which exists concretely. We cannot hold it with our hands or look at it with our eyes or dissect it with our intellect. Even the fully realized victorious ones do not see it as a concrete thing. This automatically clears away the extreme view of existence, of eternalism. On the other hand, this mind essence is the basis for all of samsara and nirvana to take place, and is not complete nothingness like space. It is not nonexistent. To understand this fact makes the view of nihilism fall apart.

This verse is extremely important. When we try to examine our mind, what do we find? We do not find a 'thing' which we can think of or perceive. Beyond being an object of investigation it is not existent, and therefore lies beyond the extreme of existence, of eternalism. But on the other hand, we have various sorts of feelings and thoughts, as well as our sense organs, which link objects and consciousness together. Different sense perceptions occur; we see forms, hear sounds and so forth. So because of perception, mind is not nonexistent. In this way the extreme of the mind as a complete nothing is also avoided.

Song of Karmapa

Usually we perceive our world as very real and concrete, full of mountains and houses and roads. Our habit of holding on in this way makes the world seem very solid. But if we closely examine our perceptions, we find that experience occurs, yet it is devoid of any self-entity. In other words, the mind is beyond the extremes of both existence and nonexistence.

These two facts, that it is not existent since even the victorious ones do not see it, and that it is not nonexistent since it is the basis of samsara and nirvana, do not contradict each other. They are co-existent, inseparable aspects, like water and its liquidity, fire and its heat, like a flower and its smell or sandalwood and its scent.

Mind is not existent since even the perfectly enlightened ones, the buddhas who see everything in the three times distinctly and precisely, have not seen it as being a concrete thing of a certain size, color or shape. Therefore we cannot say that the mind exists. But as the basis of samsara and nirvana, in the sense that its nature is to manifest perception, thoughts and feelings, we cannot say it is nonexistent. There is no contradiction or conflict here. That is the view of the Middle Way. Samsara is not understanding the unity of the two truths; nirvana is having the right understanding of this unity. This is the dividing line between samsara and nirvana.

The two aspects of existence and nonexistence are not in contradiction. Our intellect cannot usually conceive of something which 'is' and 'isn't' simultaneously. Because we think either "it is" or "it is not!", existence, and nonexistence seem to contradict one another, but actually they do not. The nature of mind is something which both 'is' and 'is not' at the same time. That is the Middle Way of unity. Middle Way means free from the extremes of 'is' and 'is not,' the extremes of eternalism and nihilism. But it is also free from the middle. There is not some separate 'middle' to grasp.

Song of Karmapa

The last line is the aspiration or wish to realize the nature of mind free from extremes. We cannot find the end of space in any direction: east, west, north, south, above or below. The nature of mind is like space, totally free from any limitation or partiality. The nature of our mind, which is the basic wakefulness of all the victorious ones, the buddhas of the three times — this is what we want to realize, and quite soon, not after a long time.

Nothing can illustrate it by the statement, "this is it."
No one can deny it by saying "it is not this."
This nature transcending concepts is unconditioned.
May we realize this view of the true meaning.

The meaning of this verse is the same as that of the previous one. In colloquial Tibetan, important points are repeatedly emphasized. If we want a friend to do something for us we could just hint at it. However, if we repeat a few times, "Please please do this for me, don't forget it!" because of our emphasis, our friend will keep our request in mind for at least a day. It will be impossible to forget. This is the way these teachings are presented here.

Nothing can illustrate it by the statement, "this is it'," or "it is not this." Various words can point out or illustrate the nature of mind: we can say it is dharmakaya, mind essence, dharmadhatu, ordinary mind, innate wakefulness, self-existing awareness and so forth. There are many words to use, all supposed to express something. Yet words are insufficient to point out what the nature of our experience really is. Ultimate truth is beyond conceptual mind. 'Coemergent wisdom,' 'innate wakefulness' or any other name we may use all point beyond conceptual mind. It is therefore impossible to realize mind nature by conceptual constructs and arguments.

We can only understand these lines from the perspective of meditation experience. The words are about

Song of Karmapa

the experience of the innate nature that lies beyond extremes. To reiterate, when saying that no analogy can be used to say "this is it!", the meaning is that no example or statement can completely show the natural state of Mahamudra.

Similarly, no one can deny it, saying "it is not this." Just as we fail to find an analogy to demonstrate Mahamudra, we also cannot disclaim any state of mind saying, "Mahamudra is something separate from this." Any attempt to affirm or deny lies within conceptual thinking. "This is it!" is a conceptual thought and "This is not it!" is equally conceptual. It is not enough to claim that the natural state of unconditioned luminosity is like space, and yet we cannot find a superior analogy. Consequently, when we are faced with the task of establishing what the natural state really is, we have no other alternative than asserting that it is indescribable — beyond the limitations of is and is not, right and wrong. Any category into which we try to define the natural state falls short of being the indescribable nature.

Using any analogy is imperfect, but at the same time not using one is also imperfect. In short, the innate, natural state cannot be defined in any way; it lies beyond the reach of philosophy. Any philosophical point of view, no matter how subtle or lucid, is by nature conceptual: it cannot be asserted and maintained without a conceptual frame of mind. This is also why we often hear it said that the view of Mahamudra and Dzogchen transcends philosophy.

The important point here is that a philosophical point of view must first of all be logically established by means of intelligent proof. But in this context that which we attempt to prove lies beyond an object that can be established. That which proves or establishes is necessarily conceptual mind, and conceptual thinking cannot establish that which transcends concepts.

The bottom line is that conceptual mind can never logically establish the total absence of all types of conceptual attitudes. This is why the Buddha uttered, "Since I don't assert, I am utterly flawless!" We must understand here that any philosophical point of view, no matter how impressive, is always imperfect since it is nothing but a point of view. This is also why some Westerners say that they don't like to be pigeonholed within a philosophical box.

To tell the truth, everything included within samsara, nirvana and the path is stamped with the seal of Mahamudra. The nature of all phenomena is Mahamudra but their modes of appearing differ between confusion and liberation. Phrased in the terminology of the lower vehicles, all phenomena without exception are empty and devoid of a self-entity. The Mahamudra teachings say that all phenomena are embraced by or have the nature of the unconstructed single sphere of dharmakaya. Thus, no one can deny it, saying "it is not this."

Buddha nature transcends concepts and is unconditioned. Unconditioned means that which does not arise, remain or cease. Anything which first arises, exists for sometime and then disappears is conditioned. The views of Mahamudra, Dzogchen and Madhyamika are said to be always free from mental fabrication, beyond constructs. But what does it mean, 'to transcend' or 'to be beyond'? It means that the moment of resting in the view is free from grasping. If we think "I am resting in emptiness," we are not beyond concepts. Thinking "I am meditating upon emptiness" is also not beyond concepts. Transcending concepts is to be totally free from both gross and subtle notions, from both having an idea about mind and from investigating its nature. One has erred if one has the slightest grasping, fixation or fascination. In Dzogchen, the moment of transcending concepts is called cutting through.

Song of Karmapa

Without realizing this, we circle through the ocean of samsara.
When realizing it, buddhahood is not somewhere else.
It is completely devoid of "it is this" or "it is not this."
May we see this vital point of the all-ground, the nature of things.

Without realizing the nature of mind which is free from extremes, from words, or from the terms existence and nonexistence, and in which emptiness and dependent origination are a unity, we circle through the ocean of samsara.

Without realizing the meaning of the key point of the nature of mind, samsara continues endlessly. If we do realize the nature of mind, then this process is reversed and buddhahood eventually results. When we have pure perception then our environment itself is a buddha realm and we ourselves are buddhas. Since the nature of mind is primordially the buddha nature, this enlightened essence permeates everywhere. It is completely devoid of anything which we can point to and about which we can say "it is this" or "it is not this."

Things appear in that they are perceived, while in fact they are by nature nonexistent. While being empty or nonexistent they still appear, and this occurs without any contradictions or conflict between emptiness and appearance. This nature of things is what we must realize. May we see the vital point of the nature of things, the unity of appearance and emptiness.

At this point we should add that all phenomena, all things, appear or come into being through interdependent arising and are therefore also empty. If they were not empty, they would not be dependent upon any other thing in order to appear. As Nagarjuna said: "I have never seen any phenomena that did not originate without the interdependence of cause and effect; therefore I have never seen any phenomena that is not empty." With this in mind we will have a good understanding of what is meant by the emptiness of things, that there is not a single thing which arises independently. Therefore there is not a single thing that is not empty. Emptiness is not something beyond or different from dependent origination, nor is dependent origination something above or below emptiness. The 'nature of things' and the 'all-ground' both refer to suchness — the indivisible unity of emptiness and dependent origination. May we understand this vital point.

Questions and Answers

Student: I have always found the idea of phenomena as dependent arising difficult to understand. The only way that I can even come close to understanding what we are talking about is by using the example of an image of two things happening simultaneously in a mirror. Could you comment on that?

Rinpoche: We must simply understand the difference between relative and ultimate reality; the way things seem and the way they really are. All things arise in interdependence. In the way they seem, mountains, houses, people and so forth do exist. But when examined as to the way they really are, they are found to be empty of reality or any kind of independent substance; there is nothing which can stand alone. Everything is relative to something else: White is relative to black, big to small and so forth. If we examine closely, we do not find anything which is independent; that is how things really are. But they appear as all the experiences and phenomena of the six realms. From the perspective of the six realms, the six kinds of beings do exist, just as all the different kinds of pleasure and pain do exist. There is cause and effect of actions, there is karma. But in essence none of these exist; actually there are no six realms, no beings and no karma.

Student: What was meant by the line "It is not nonexistent?"

Rinpoche: You are referring to the lines: "It is not existent since even the victorious ones do not see it. It is not nonexistent since it is the basis of samsara and nirvana." Why is the nature of mind not nonexistent? Given the possibility of perception, of experience taking place, we cannot say that it is nonexistent. For example, based on the buddha nature you can prove that the mind is the unity of emptiness and cognizance. Whether we call it 'relative phenomena,' 'the cognizance of enlightened mind' or 'the apparent aspect of things,' still there is something that cannot be denied, and this refers not only to mistaken mind. But when we examine a thought or feeling, there is no concrete thing to find; it has no self nature. We have arrived at emptiness.

We experience this sometimes when we just sit down without trying to do anything, without thinking. Suddenly a kind of keen and alert wakefulness occurs by itself. That shows that mind is not nonexistent. As the Buddha said in the sutras, "Mind is not the dualistic mind, it is its cognizant nature."

Student: You said that the dharmakaya is with us all the time, so we should try to realize it quickly. I want to know how we can begin to acknowledge this if we cannot rely on concepts? You said that any words which are used to describe it are just names. How can we perceive the dharmakaya in our ordinary life if it is always present, yet ignored?

Rinpoche: Without relying on words we will not be able to understand the ultimate, but clinging to words will also keep us from understanding. Many great scholars who were too fascinated with words and concepts failed to attain realization. Maybe their great interest in logic and debate kept them from it. On the other hand, it is very difficult to approach an understanding of dharmakaya without using words. Clear use of well-chosen

Song of Karmapa

words dispels confusion and avoids complications. Although words are very important, clinging to them does not bring ultimate benefit.

How can we realize dharmakaya quickly? According to the Mahamudra and Dzogchen systems, we should find a qualified master and receive the four empowerments from him. We should understand what is being pointed out, what insight we are being empowered to possess. At that point the wisdom mind of the teacher is somehow transmitted. In this way it is possible to be introduced to basic wakefulness and to experience it.

Once the view has been pointed out and recognized, the next step is to sustain it through meditation training. There are basically two kinds of approach to meditation practice. One is called 'analytical meditation', the other simply 'resting meditation.' In analytical meditation, you receive teachings on a certain text, and investigate the assertions with a critical mind from beginning to end. Think "Are these statements really right or not?", "Why are they valid?", "Why not?" Really think about it. That is the scholarly approach of analytical meditation.

The other approach is applied when a qualified master meets a qualified student. The student follows the teacher and receives teachings, just as Milarepa followed Marpa and Naropa followed Tilopa. The connection between teacher and student should be based on the student's complete trust in the teacher and confidence in the teaching. The master should have great kindness towards the student, more than towards his own son or daughter. Then the pointing-out instruction, the real transmission, can take place. You may have heard how Tilopa pointed out the nature of Mahamudra to Naropa by slapping him on the side of his face with a shoe. It can happen like that. There are many other stories of unusual ways of having the nature of mind pointed out, such as through beatings or other strange means of indication. Sometimes when the master and student simply sit together, the student can

Song of Karmapa

recognize the nature through his great devotion to the master. Having had the nature 'pointed out,' to rest in that nature is called 'resting meditation.'

The words 'to trust' or 'have faith' seem too simple at first glance. What is the use of having a high appreciation of somebody else? Basically, trust creates moments of openness. Having such trust from the core of our heart makes us like an open flower. In the moment of faith the wisdom of realization can be transmitted as a blessing. This means that in that moment of openness one can realize the wisdom mind of the teacher. This is the most important link between student and master, and can occur between a master with great compassion and realization and a student who is completely open, who has trust and faith. Other types of connection, such as that between a master who needs money and a wealthy student, are not enough for wisdom or realization to take place. Merely handing over a sum of money does not guarantee that authentic transmission will occur.

Student: I have a question about such transmission. If the student has that openness and sees the master as a real emanation but the master is not actually realized, will transmission still take place?

Rinpoche: That is difficult. The master as well as the student must be qualified. If a qualified student has a really sincere wish to realize the nature of mind and connects with an unqualified teacher, he is not very clever.

Student: What is the difference or the link between the general word 'samadhi' and the view of Mahamudra?

Rinpoche: The late Kunu Rinpoche said that 'sama' (*ting-nge* in Tibetan), which means 'state' or 'continuum,' is like the continuity of sound that persists for a certain duration after you strike a bell. 'Dhi' (*dzin* in Tibetan), means 'to hold' in the sense of 'adhering to' or 'resting in' that continuous state of composure. There is not necessarily any difference between that idea and the view of Mahamudra, although the word samadhi can be used in many different contexts and has different meanings in other places.

QUESTION: Another more traditional sense for the word samadhi is defined as 'focusing one-pointedly upon a mental image.' Is that then the same as the view of Mahamudra?

Rinpoche: No, it is not, because that connotation of samadhi refers to shamatha practice in which one focuses on one thing in order to keep the mind still. This is different from the view in the context of Mahamudra.

Rather, we should use the phrase 'nonconceptual samadhi', which leads away from the idea of samadhi as holding one-pointedly to a thing. The 'nonconceptual' removes the 'holding', bringing us closer to the Mahamudra view. This nonconceptual samadhi is not the same as the samadhi of shamatha practice. It is a self-sustained spontaneous state which occurs after having arrived at nonconceptual wakefulness. Once you have arrived at that, there is no difference between Mahamudra, Dzogchen or Madhyamika. In that context the word 'samadhi' connotes 'equanimity,' a word often translated into English as 'meditation.' However, the ordinary meaning of meditation is not applicable here.

Mahamudra has different divisions. The three main ones are sutra Mahamudra, tantric Mahamudra, and essence Mahamudra. The last is also called 'Mahamudra devoid of constructs'. The first is described in *The Jewel Ornament of Liberation*, which is based on quotes from the sutras. Tantric Mahamudra involves practices with the channels, energies and essences, which in Sanskrit are known as *nadi, prana* and *bindu*. Essence Mahamudra means being introduced to the naked nature of your mind and is exactly the same as Dzogchen. Longchenpa and Mipham Rinpoche have both declared this, as have many other masters.

The usual idea of 'meditation' can lead to misunderstanding when talking about Mahamudra. Usually the word 'meditate' means to ponder or reflect upon a particular mental image, either a tantric image with multiple faces and arms and different colors holding objects in its hands, or a certain idea such as compassion, impermanence or emptiness that we think of and try to grow accustomed to. 'Meditation' implies a meditator who meditates upon an object. However, this has very little to do with Mahamudra practice, so we must use other terms such as 'nonmeditation' to show that the practice is without the three concepts of a meditator, a meditation object, and the act of meditating. 'Undistracted nonmeditation' is the most commonly used term in the different manuals of Mahamudra practice. This key term indicates exactly how to practice. 'Nonmeditation' implies that the practice is not to sit and think of something.

Mahamudra is not only not to meditate upon an object, but also not to be distracted. What is nondistraction? In ordinary daily life nondistraction means not to forget what you are doing. Nonmeditation means not to forget the unfabricated state of naked mind. At the time of nonmeditation, remain only in that and don't be distracted from it. Conceptual mind has no work here. Although concepts are very important for the development stage, we do not need them in the completion stage. We must totally abandon conceptual mind. The completion stage is the time of undistracted nonmeditation. Nonmeditation means that there is not even a speck of dust upon which to meditate. Grow accustomed to the fact that there is nothing upon which to meditate. This is the meditation training of Mahamudra.

This meditation training is free of thoughts of the three times. All the instruction manuals say, "Do not follow after thoughts of the past; do not invite thoughts of the future; and whatever present thoughts occur, do not conceptualize and do not examine." Not to follow after gross or subtle thoughts, also called *tokpa* and *chöpa*, conceiving and discerning, is called nonmeditation. This is the supreme type of meditation.

Nondistraction and nonmeditation are the two vital points mentioned in all the meditation manuals. The *Bodhicharya Avatara* also says, "Without knowing the key point of mind, joys, and sorrows naturally follow and whatever we do will be pointless." The key point of mind for Shantideva is undistracted nonmeditation.

At first, this sounds very strange and contradictory. First the teacher says "You must meditate, you should practice." We have heard this hundreds of times. Then suddenly we hear the word 'nonmeditation' which sounds like 'do not meditate.' We might become confused and say, "Forget it; I will just do nothing." But it does not mean to abandon the training. Try to understand correctly. 'Nonmeditation' means not to hold certain concepts in mind, and to not be distracted from the absence of holding concepts.

Gyalwa Götsangpa said: "My master told me to go to the mountain and meditate. I have meditated and meditated but now I do not find any meditation — what shall I do?" Through practicing the teachings he discovered there was no meditator and no real thing to meditate upon. He arrived at the ultimate view

4

CUTTING THROUGH MISCONCEPTIONS

Perceiving is mind, being empty is also mind.
Realizing is mind, being mistaken is also mind.
Having arisen is mind, having ceased is also mind.
May we cut through all our doubts concerning mind.

The phrase 'perceiving is mind' means that through the different senses, the mind perceives form, sound, smells and so forth. The mental faculty also perceives all the different thoughts and emotions. At the same time, however, all these perceptions and experiences are empty, as is mind. Since the mind can perceive, we cannot say it is nonexistent, but because the perceptions are empty, the extreme of existence is cleared away.

The next lines say, "Realizing is mind, being mistaken is also mind. Having arisen is mind, having ceased is also mind." We must understand that mind is most important; everything is based on mind. Our actions of body and speech depend upon our mind. If we can control the mind, our words and actions are automatically controlled. To do this we must cut through all doubts about mind, by relying on the three kinds of knowledge resulting from learning, reflection, and meditation. If we undertake these we will display the signs of learning, which are being disciplined and gentle, and the sign of meditation practice, which is having fewer disturbing emotions.

What are doubts concerning mind? In order to truly understand the mind and dispel doubt we must discuss 'ground and ground manifestation,' our basic nature and its manifestations. Our basic nature itself is undeluded, unmistaken. Delusion occurs the instant our basic nature manifests. At that moment, we confuse this event with a 'self' and 'other,' 'me' and 'that.' There has never been any confusion at all in the ground itself; confusion occurs in the moment of the manifestation of the ground. Although the nature itself has not the slightest confusion, ignorance of this natural state which is our own essence, causes confusion. This initial confusion is called coemergent ignorance.

Because of this coemergent ignorance the mind turns to face outward, away from its essence. It begins to conceptualize and follow after thoughts, to create negative emotions and karma, and to roam through the mentally created samsaric realms of existence. This aspect of conceptualization is called conceptual ignorance.

The traditional analogy for this process of confusion is mistaking a coiled rope for a snake. At first glance, a coiled rope lying in semi-darkness or in tall grass might appear to be a snake. The rope has no power of its own to cause fear, but we become frightened due to the confusion which arises in our mind. This initial error in perception is the basis for both hope and fear, and we think, "I wish this snake would go away," or "Maybe it will bite me!" Because of our mistake we entertain hope and fear, and thus we suffer.

Look at the course our mistaken perception has followed. We initially apprehend the perceiver as being a subject, an 'I.' Next, we apprehend that which is perceived as being an object, the 'other' or 'not-self.' The nonexistent is apprehended as existent and the false is held to be true. Impure is perceived as pure, while the pure dharmakaya is perceived as impure. Ignoring our own nature, we fall prey to distraction and are carried away by confusion. At that point we can no longer remain stable in our innate wakefulness. We become attached and cling to this confused state of mind and grow accustomed to it. From then on our experience is continually apprehended in a totally mistaken way as subject and object. Based on this perverted dualistic fixation we engage in unwholesome ways of acting and accumulate negative karma. We have been going through this since beginningless time. The effect of this accumulated negative karma is illusory experience, the joys and sorrows of the six realms. Continuing to experience in this deluded way, we suffer the results of our own actions.

We can understand this in the context of the three aspects of ground, path, and fruition Mahamudra. Ground Mahamudra refers to the recognition of what we already have, the ground or buddha nature. Recognition of this at the moment of pointing-out by our teacher is called ground Mahamudra. Milarepa and Gampopa have said that Mahamudra is the nature which is neither existent nor nonexistent, which is not limited in any way by an extreme point of view, which is not improved by enlightenment nor worsened by wandering in samsara, and which is never confused or liberated. We already have the ground but have failed to acknowledge it.

Path Mahamudra is the effort made through training to develop this recognition and to become more and more stable in it. Finally fruition Mahamudra is the end, the ultimate result of having attained whatever is to be attained, having cleared away all that should be cleared away and having abandoned whatever should be abandoned.

Having recognized innate wakefulness, we must not leave it at that. Each time we recognize our nature the temporary confusion vanishes and our innate wisdom is

Song of Karmapa

automatically present. We must train in this and thereby attain stability. Lack of recognition is the main cause for continuing in samsara. This ignorance causes disturbing emotions which accumulate negative karma. The main difference between a sentient being and an enlightened one lies in these two aspects: knowing and not knowing, knowledge and ignorance, confusion and nonconfusion. Thus may we cut through all our doubts concerning mind.

Unspoiled by intellectual and deliberate meditation,
And unmoved by the winds of ordinary distractions,
May we be skilled in sustaining the practice of mind
  essence,
Being able to rest in unfabricated and innate
  naturalness.

This four-line verse contains three steps: first, how to begin meditation practice, second, how to actually rest in meditative composure, and third, how to sustain this state continuously. We begin the meditation practice with the second line, "Unmoved by the winds of ordinary distractions." Various outer, inner and secret obstacles may prevent us from engaging in meditation practice. In general there are the eight worldly concerns, beginning with being happy when we obtain something and being unhappy when we do not. This can be food or clothes or anything in the world; when we have it we become very excited, but when we lack it or lose it, we become very depressed. The next two worldly concerns are being happy when meeting something pleasant, be it a pleasant form, sound, taste, smell, or texture, and being unhappy when something unpleasant appears. The third set of worldly concerns is being happy when we are famous and unhappy when we are not. The fourth set of worldly concerns is being happy when praised and unhappy when blamed. If someone says "You have very beautiful eyes," immediately we feel very pleased, while if they add "but your nose is crooked," we feel like crying. We instinctively have these mundane reactions; they are not something we have been taught. Already from birth we instinctively like gain, pleasure, fame and praise.

The eight worldly concerns are hindrances to meditation practice. Most people fall under their influence and as a result experience much suffering. Attachment to good name, one's neighbors, one's country and so on are the source of many problems. Influenced by these eight worldly concerns we are carried away by the three major disturbing emotions, and great trouble ensues. For the practitioner these emotions cause many obstacles or demons to arise so that we are prevented from doing what is meaningful and worthwhile. When actually engaging in meditation training we face more subtle obstacles, such as feeling obscured, dull or drowsy. These distractions which carry us away are likened to the wind, because they move or disturb the mind. "Unmoved" means refraining from being governed by such distractions. The Bodhisattva Shantideva said in his *Bodhicharya Avatara*: "When dwelling in secluded mountains one hears only the melodious sounds of birds and running water. There is nothing to upset your mind, so adhere to quiet places!"

The second point is to be unspoiled by intellectual and deliberate meditation. When beginning to practice, assume the seven-fold posture of Vairochana, a traditional meditation posture. Your state of mind should be unspoiled by the intellectual, the mind-made and the deliberate. Meditation which tries to create something of itself only spoils or distorts the view of Mahamudra which is to allow the presence of ordinary, natural mind. This is very important, a vital point.

'Intellectual' or 'mind-made' means to sit and think "My mind essence is empty! At the same time its nature is cognizant, luminous! These two are naturally a unity!" To sit and think consciously of these two aspects is called intellectual meditation. Deliberate meditation is

Song of Karmapa

trying to keep our mind focused or concentrated one-pointedly on a certain idea, trying to create the natural state.

Intellectually making an assumption that the mind is such and such and clinging to that, or trying to create a state of mind through effort or deliberation, are both, faults that will only spoil the view of Mahamudra. The correct and genuine practice is the opposite of mind-made meditation: resting in unfabricated and innate naturalness, as expressed in the fourth line.

The *Prajnaparamita of 70,000 Verses* says: "Not trying to reject, hold on to or accept any attribute, that is the view of Prajnaparamita; that is the meditation of Prajnaparamita." Not to hold anything in mind, not to construct anything mentally: that is the view of Prajnaparamita, transcendent knowledge. The meditation of Prajnaparamita is to not meditate on anything whatsoever. The Kagyü system of Mahamudra says, "Without inviting the future, without following the past, without trying to correct or alter the present, simply rest in natural and ordinary mind without fabricating anything." That is what is explained by the fourth line.

Listen well to this explanation by the Lord of Dharma, Gampopa: "What does it mean not to follow the past? It means that we do not chase after thoughts about the past. Not to invite the future means that we do not prepare for or anticipate the future. Not to alter the present means we do not try to think deliberately of anything whatsoever".

By allowing our attention to run after thoughts of past, present or future we become involved with the five poisons, perform various karmic actions and continue to wander in samsara. By resting in the unmodified, unchanged nature pointed out by our master, we recognize the empty essence and cognizant nature and realize the ground wisdom which is like clear, undisturbed water. Mahasiddha Saraha said: "At all times let your mind rest in nonaction in the state of innate naturalness, without trying to create anything. That I proclaim to be the meditation."

"Rest in unfabricated and innate naturalness." 'Unfabricated' and 'innate' are the key words in Mahamudra. To rest in naturalness means not to follow the thoughts of past, present and future. Resting in naturalness itself is what we call ordinary mind, self-existing wakefulness. It has many names. It is also called buddha nature.

The aspiration is to become skilled in sustaining the practice of the mind essence. 'Mind' here means that which knows or experiences all the joys and sorrows, all the different emotions. It is mind which attains enlightenment, and it is also mind which roams confused in samsaric existence. May we become skilled in understanding exactly what this mind is, through learning, contemplation and meditation. As Shantideva has said: "If one does not know the key point of mind, one cannot avoid suffering; one cannot attain happiness even if one desires to do so. But if one knows the key point of mind, suffering is automatically avoided and happiness is automatically gained."

Questions and Answers

Student: How do you clear away the states of being obscured or agitated?

Rinpoche: Meditation practice manuals discuss this. Strong devotion to your teacher, compassion towards sentient beings and an acute sense of presence of mind can clear these away. Because the view is without anything to be cleared away or to be established, the best practice is simply to remain in the view. When this is not possible, to help you to simply rest you can rely on 'clearing away practices' such as cultivating devotion and compassion.

Song of Karmapa

Student: What is the difference between Mahamudra according to the sutras, Mahamudra according to the tantras, and essence Mahamudra?

Rinpoche: There is no difference whatsoever in the view because the view is simplicity, free from any mental constructs. But there are differences in the meditation and how to approach the view. Following the sutra system, one goes through shamatha and vipashyana and then progresses through the paths and levels. Tantric Mahamudra entails the yogic exercises and the Six Doctrines of Naropa. Essence Mahamudra is identical with Dzogchen practice in the sense that it is simple and without any elaborations. It is very direct.

Student: How do we train in the practice of Mahamudra?

Rinpoche: After receiving the essential instructions from a qualified master we must clearly distinguish between two aspects: *namtog* and *nampar mitogpa*, conceptual thinking and the absence of conceptual thinking. The absence of conceptual thinking is the naked state of nondual awareness called *rigpa* in Tibetan. When we think "I am going to practice Mahamudra," that is a concept. When we look back afterwards and think "I practiced Mahamudra and it went well," or "It did not go well," again we are involved in conceptual thinking. While practicing we must be free from thoughts of wanting to practice Mahamudra or that we are practicing Mahamudra. Concepts such as "Now I am meditating. It is going quite well," "My meditation is no good," "Now I lost it!" or "Now I've got it!", are all mistaken. We need to free ourselves from all these thoughts. To practice while avoiding all conceptualization is to truly maintain the continuity of Mahamudra.

So what is the state of Mahamudra like? It is indescribable and inconceivable, in the same way that the taste of sugar is totally inexpressible for a mute. If we must give some explanation, it is like this: in the state of

Song of Karmapa

Mahamudra the five sense perceptions are totally free and unblocked. We do not black out or experience a blank nothingness; neither do we fixate on objects as being one way or another. Mahamudra can only be described as a state of being vividly awake, clear, lucid and empty. We cannot say much else about Mahamudra. It is truly beyond words. The main point is to learn to be free from conceptualizing. The correct view is without fixation or clinging. If these two faults are present, we do not have the genuine view of Mahamudra.

Right now we may think that unless we meditate or do something, we will not attain the state of Mahamudra, just as a bell will not ring unless we take it in our hand and shake it. We want to do *something* to make the state of Mahamudra happen, but it is not like that. Most importantly we need mindfulness — a kind of 'remindfulness' — to remind us of the practice. No matter what you are doing, whether formally sitting on your meditation cushion, walking about, eating, talking, washing or lying down, suddenly remember the practice of Mahamudra. That remembrance should bring you to the state of Mahamudra. In that instant do not hold onto anything; the total absence of clinging and fixation is itself the state of Mahamudra. In the very moment of no fixation there is also no confusion. With no confusion, there are no disturbing emotions and no accumulation of karma. In a moment of anger, for example, we always fixate on an object and attach the anger to it. Without this mental attachment to an object, the anger has no basis on which to occur or be sustained. The moment we let go of clinging to or fixating on the object, there is no place for the anger to remain.

"First one needs thought, then one needs non-thought." We must first remember to practice, but during the actual training we should be totally free from any concepts. Meditation mingled with conceptualization is not genuine Mahamudra but just an imitation. The state of Mahamudra is actually extremely simple and very close to oneself, but because of the habitual pattern of always grasping and fixating on things, what should be easy has become difficult.

Student: Should we wear down conceptual mind with lots of examination, investigation and visualization so that the state of Mahamudra can surface?

Rinpoche: Vajrayana is characterized as having many methods and few hardships. It is said, "The path of fabrication leads to naturalness." The whole point of the many different Vajrayana practices is to lead us in the right direction. The development stage of visualizing deities with bodies of rainbow light exhausts the mind's habit of grasping to and solidifying things. The mind then becomes more free and open and it is easier for realization to dawn. Faith, resting in equanimity, or making supplications for the blessings of compassion, wisdom and the enlightened abilities to enter ourselves all work in the same way. As our karmic obscurations begin to thin out through practice, recognizing innate wakefulness becomes easier.

Student: I would like to ask how to mingle ordinary life, Dharma practice and the practice of Mahamudra.

Rinpoche: There are different approaches to this. A person of the highest capacity who is both very intelligent and diligent need not go elsewhere or do anything other than what he is already doing. The practice can be mingled with any activity; not only during daily life, walking and eating and talking and so on, but also you can dissolve into the luminosity of deep sleep. Those who are not of the highest capacity should always do their best to remind themselves of the practice in all situations. That is the idea of mindfulness, always to remind yourself of the practice. Be mindful of the practice at all times during the day.

Some people feel extremely uncomfortable when they are meditating sitting down. Even more thoughts arise, so it becomes almost impossible for them to sit, but if they get up and slowly walk around they find they are able to practice. In some traditions, such as Japanese traditions, one alternates practice between sitting and walking. But the most important point that we hear again and again, both in the teachings and in the practice manuals, is the need to train briefly but repeatedly. The authentic natural state does not last long when we are beginning practitioners. It is very short and therefore it must be repeated many times in order for us to become familiar with it. That does not mean that people who experience the natural state for longer periods must cut it short, but rather that it should not be artificially prolonged. Practice short sessions, repeatedly.

5

EXPERIENCE AND REALIZATION

The waves of gross and subtle thoughts having
  spontaneously subsided,
The river of unwavering mind naturally abides.
Free from the stains of dullness, sluggishness and
  conceptualization,
May we be stable in the unmoving ocean of shamatha.

The first line of this verse explains the combined practices of shamatha and vipashyana, mentioning gross and subtle thoughts. According to Abhidharma, 'gross' refers to a rough idea about something; 'subtle' is precise discernment. The gross perception of an outer object comes first, followed by the precise discernment; based on these, the fifty-one mental states arise. Both gross and subtle thoughts are likened to ripples or waves on the surface of water. When they are allowed to subside spontaneously, the mind, meaning the all-ground consciousness, will abide unwaveringly like the flow of a river.

Being 'free from the stains of dullness, sluggishness and conceptualization, may we be stable in the unmoving ocean of shamatha.' The text specifically mentions the two flaws of dullness and sluggishness, but condensed into these are all the others, including agitation, regret, doubt, ill-will, sleepiness, desire and craving. Many teachings provide instruction on methods for clearing away these defects. Rangjung Dorje continues:

When looking again and again into the unseen mind,
The fact that there is nothing to see is vividly seen as it is.
Cutting through doubts about its nature being existent or nonexistent
May we unmistakenly recognize our own essence.

The view is without the act of viewing, and the mind which is seen is beyond something seen. Not trying to see a particular thing, simply rest evenly in the nature of mind and sustain its continuity, adhering to the oral instruction of your master. Look again and again with the eye of knowledge.

The fact that there is no seer and nothing to see is vividly seen as it is. 'Vividly seen' is a play on the word vipashyana which means 'seeing clearly'. By cutting through any doubts and misconceptions about whether it is existent or nonexistent, like this or not like this or like something else, may we clearly and unmistakenly recognize our own essence and may the innate wakefulness of vipashyana dawn.

This is an aspiration to realize 'ordinary mind,' co-emergent wisdom, wakefulness free from extremes. May we recognize the nature of mind which is free from all kinds of statements we can make about it, and beyond mental constructs such as 'it is' or 'it is not.' Although empty, it is not a blank void; although luminous, it does not shine with a light. May we recognize this nature of mind directly; may we attain this certainty.

The true meaning is not some object which is to be held as a reference point; nor is it something to be viewed or meditated upon. It is the experience of our own self-cognizant wakefulness. May we realize this ground wisdom.

Song of Karmapa

The *Condensed Prajnaparamita* mentions that sentient beings say "I see space," but if asked "How do you see it?", they cannot say anything because there is nothing to say. Likewise, ground wisdom, which is the unity of being empty and cognizant, can be experienced by oneself, but cannot be expressed in words. As the following lines praising the *Prajnaparamita* indicate:

> Transcendent knowledge is inexpressible,
>   inconceivable and beyond description.
> Nonarising and unceasing like the essence of
>   space,
> It is experienced by self-cognizant wakefulness.
> I pay homage to this mother of the buddhas of
>   the three times.

The *Aspiration of Mahamudra* further elucidates the view of emptiness:

When observing objects, they are seen to be the mind,
  devoid of objects.
When observing the mind, there is no mind, as it is
  empty of an entity.
When observing both, dualistic fixation is spontaneously
  freed.
May we realize the natural state of the luminous mind.

The phrase 'when observing objects,' refers to sense objects: the forms we see with our eyes, the sounds we hear with our ears, and the tastes, smells and textures we perceive with our other senses. 'Observing' here means resting in meditative composure and looking from the state of an even mind. In this state we realize that objects possess no independent identity, no substantial existence. Things are naturally empty and their identity and quality depend on the perceiving mind. There are no external, self-existent objects, just cognizance, the perceiving mind.

Song of Karmapa

Just as objects lack any independent existence, when we observe the mind that perceives these objects, it too is devoid of independent existence. The mind is that which experiences sensations, thoughts, and emotions. To 'look' into this mind is not a visual act as such; it means simply resting. Resting in the state of composure according to the meditation instructions, there is no mind, no fixed entity, no substantial thing that can be found. It is naturally empty.

The word 'observing' in the third line means resting in the natural state in which the perceived objects and the mind that perceives are both of 'same taste,' of the same nature. By the power of remaining in such a state of one taste, the fixation on the duality of subject and object, of perceiver and what is perceived, is naturally freed in itself.

By understanding how to rest in this way, we realize the natural state of luminous mind, nonconceptual and self-cognizant wakefulness. This is the wisdom of vipashyana, of 'clear seeing', which dawns the same moment the obscuration of our dualistic clinging has collapsed. Here the teaching is phrased as an aspiration: "May we realize the natural state of the luminous mind." Appearances are mind. Mind is empty. Emptiness is spontaneously present, and this spontaneous presence is self-liberated. These four points are included in this verse.

Being free from mental fabrication, it is Mahamudra.
Devoid of extremes, it is the Great Middle Way.
It is also called Dzogchen, the embodiment of all.
May we attain the confidence of realizing all by knowing
  one nature.

The first line describes the view of Mahamudra as being free from mental constructs. Specifically this refers to the twelve aspects of the four yogas of Mahamudra — one-pointedness, simplicity, one taste and nonmeditation — about which much can be said. To sum up the essence, however, coemergent wisdom or natural wakefulness is free of all mental fabrications and formulations that can be made about it. Therefore Mahamudra, also called coemergent wisdom, innate wakefulness or ordinary mind, is said to be free from mental constructs, assumptions or fabrications.

Buddhist teachings sometimes express one meaning by different words or names. For example, Mahamudra, Madhyamika and Dzogchen all teach the same essence, but have different lineages, terminology and traditional approaches. Thus, people who practice Madhyamika say the view described above is the Madhyamika view, whereas Mahamudra followers call it the view of Mahamudra and practitioners of Dzogchen call it the Dzogchen view.

Madhyamika, the 'Great Middle,' says the view is devoid of extremes and constructs. 'Extremes' are the extreme of existence, nonexistence, both and neither, the eight complexities, the extremes of exaggeration and denigration, being and not being and so forth. Freedom from all of these extremes is what the great Middle Way, Madhyamika, postulates. This great Madhyamika of unity refers to either the unity of the two truths or the unity which is beyond the extremes of existence and nonexistence, both and neither.

When one first hears this it is a little difficult to grasp. What is something which neither exists nor does not exist? By negating nihilism it avoids falling into some kind of blank or void, while by being something nonexistent, it avoids falling into the view of eternalism. At first glance this may seem confusing but on further investigation it appears very reasonable and very straightforward, and extremely beneficial. That is the view of Madhyamika.

These three terms, the Great Middle, Mahamudra, and Dzogchen, all connote greatness. Madhyamika, the 'Great Middle,' is called 'middle' because it does not fall into the extreme viewpoints of eternalism or nihilism. It adheres to the great middle path of unity beyond constructs. As the most eminent or supreme method for conquering disturbing emotions, it is 'great.'

'Maha' means 'great' and 'mudra' means 'seal,' signifying that all phenomena have the 'seal' of emptiness. Since it is a most profound or very high view set forth to conquer disturbing emotions, it is called 'great.'

Likewise, Dzogchen, the Great Perfection, means that all apparent and existent phenomena included within samsara and nirvana are perfect or complete within the primordially pure space of awareness. It is 'great' because there is no more profound or higher view than this for subduing disturbing emotions.

"May we attain the confidence of realizing all by knowing one nature." Traditionally there are different ways to gain this confidence of realization. The gradual way involves studying all the different sections of scriptures; Vinaya, Logic, Abhidharma, Madhyamika and Prajnaparamita; reflecting on the teachings, and gradually coming to some conclusion. The other approach is for those who are gifted like King Indrabodhi and can attain liberation simultaneous with understanding. This only works for very gifted or qualified persons who possess the karmic continuity of former practice. Realizing all by knowing one nature means we should aspire to realize the unerring view, the view of Mahamudra, Madhyamika, and Dzogchen. When a qualified teacher points out the mind essence to a qualified student who recognizes it, then all practice and teachings can be condensed into just one point. Understanding that one point, everything is vividly and clearly realized. Form the aspiration to gain the confidence of realizing all by knowing one nature. Through this view we realize 'the way it is,' the unmistaken nature of things. We pray to realize the nature of our mind.

It is said that we can 'know one hundred things but lack one.' This means that we might be very learned and know all the Kangyur, Tangyur and many instructions, but if we do not realize the perfect view, we cannot traverse the paths and bhumis and thus cannot attain buddhahood. On the other hand, without knowing all the vast treatises but recognizing the nature of the mind is called 'knowing the one point which embodies all.' After recognizing mind nature, we should train in it and gradually attain stability; thus realization happens progressively. At that point we need not rely on what others have written. The qualities of recognizing our essence as well as our capacity for exposition, debate and composition will arise unimpededly from within.

Simply having the correct view of how to recognize the mind essence will suffice for attaining enlightenment. It can be compared to crossing one hundred rivers by crossing a bridge at a point where they all flow together; a very easy thing to do. Crossing the hundred rivers one by one at places without bridges would be very difficult and time-consuming. Knowing this one vital point frees all — liberates all states of mind. This single sufficient point is the view. Realizing this, may we obtain confidence in it. Confidence is very important. This is not simply the confidence of being able to repeat what we have heard, but a deep confidence which is like being accustomed to driving a car or flying an airplane — confidence without any doubt that we can do it. An inexperienced person would feel afraid, but not one who knows how to drive or fly. Likewise, once we have attained the confidence of realization, there is no fear.

Great bliss, free from attachment, is unceasing.
Luminosity, devoid of fixation, is unobscured.
Nonthought, transcending the intellect, is spontaneously
    present.
Without effort, may our experience be unceasing.

When we practice Mahamudra meditation, certain experiences called bliss, clarity and nonthought can occur. If we cling to these experiences they become impediments, but if we are without attachment to them, they are adornments, good qualities. As Manjushri said, "If you have any clinging you do not have the correct view." Therefore, when resting in the natural state in which great bliss is unceasing, be free from attachment and fixation. 'Unceasing' here means uninterrupted.

"Luminosity, devoid of fixation, is unobscured" like the sun in a cloudless sky, totally free from cover. In the practice of Mahamudra nonthought is spontaneously present, transcending the intellect. When we experience the absence of conceptual thinking, we can either cling to it or not. Avoid holding on to or forming an intellectual idea about the experience. Make this aspiration: "Without effort, may our experience be unceasing," meaning without interruption.

To examine this in more detail, there are three kinds of experiences and their correct, pure unfolding is as follows. First is the experience of bliss, the great bliss free from attachment. When feeling blissful, have no attachment to or fascination with this experience. When there is luminosity or clarity, be free from any kind of fixation. This nongrasping state is totally unobscured. The third experience of nonthought is an absence of concepts about subject, object and action. This experience transcends the intellect and is spontaneously present. Be without any effort in the innate state, without any fabrication, without trying to deliberately produce these experiences. If they occur, do not be too excited about them. Without hope and fear, may these pure experiences be unceasing.

How can the three experiences be an impediment, something faulty? First, the habitual attachment to the sensation of bliss causes rebirth in the Realm of Desire. Second, fixating on clarity or precision can cause us to be reborn in the Realm of Form. Finally, if we cultivate the idea of absence of thought, a sustained stillness, attachment to that experience becomes the cause for taking rebirth in the Formless Realm.

Song of Karmapa

The fixation of clinging to good experiences is spontaneously freed.
The confusion of 'bad thoughts' is naturally purified.
Ordinary mind is free from acceptance and rejection.
May we realize the truth of dharmata, devoid of constructs.

If we are not fascinated by the good experiences of bliss, clarity and nonthought, then, like a knotted snake that naturally comes untied when left to itself, our grasping these experiences will be spontaneously freed. In the same way, the confusion of so-called 'bad thoughts' is naturally purified. Ordinary mind, innate wakefulness, neither accepts one thing nor rejects another. May we realize this ultimate truth of dharmata, the nature of things devoid of mental constructs.

When practicing meditation or trying to rest in the practice we may have certain experiences. We may feel extremely relaxed and comfortable, free in both body and mind. We think "Wow! Now my meditation is really good! I deeply understand the view of Mahamudra!" When this happens it is difficult not to get a little excited or exhilarated. That excitement or exhilaration is called 'clinging to the experience.' Sometimes we can experience a clarity that feels like everything is wide open, as if solid matter no longer exists and even the mountains and the earth are like open sky. Or we may have an experience of not following after any thought whatsoever, with a totally still and undisturbed mind.

Fascination with these experiences is in itself the cause for rebirth in the three realms of samsara and is not the correct view. Since wrong view brings a wrong result, abandoning attachment to any experience is therefore extremely important. How can we do that? Simply, do not get too fascinated, do not accept and indulge in these experiences; they are then naturally freed.

Song of Karmapa

Whether we have 'good thoughts' or 'bad thoughts,' they are both just thoughts. 'Thoughts' are the different mental impressions or reflections we make when we see forms, hear sounds, notice smells, tastes and textures, or recall past events. The state of neither accepting nor rejecting thought is itself called ordinary mind or basic wakefulness. That is the vital point. "May we realize the truth of dharmata, devoid of constructs."

Through such practice we stabilize the recognition of ordinary mind, our innate wakefulness free from acceptance and rejection. It is usually taught that while a practitioner is on the stage called 'path,' disturbing emotions and obscurations should be rejected and the enlightened qualities accepted and attained. But actually, in this ordinary mind which is our innate wakefulness there is nothing to accept or to reject, to discard or to attain. Ordinary mind is naturally free from anything to be discarded or achieved. May we realize this truth of dharmata, the nature of mind naturally devoid of all kinds of constructs, impermanence or permanence, coming or going, existence or nonexistence. This is the aspiration we should make.

Questions and Answers

Student: What is the difference between resting in shamatha and simply resting freely?

Rinpoche: In the context of essence Mahamudra, shamatha means simply resting in a very relaxed and free way, not being under the power of dullness or sluggishness and not following after any of the thoughts of the three times. Simply rest naturally without following thoughts. That is shamatha. Vipashyana is something more, involving acute or vivid presence of mind. The word vipashyana means to see clearly. It should be present in addition to shamatha.

The word shamatha has different meanings in different contexts. There is shamatha with focus and without focus, with object and without object. The shamatha here in essence Mahamudra is shamatha which is without reference point. Having attained a state of some stability in shamatha free from dullness and thoughts, likened here to an unmoving ocean, we need to have the vipashyana aspect pointed out. It does not happen by itself easily; it must be pointed out to us by an experienced master. But this is much easier if one has attained stability in shamatha. Therefore the Mahamudra system first teaches the importance of cultivating shamatha and then introduces the vipashyana aspect. According to Dzogchen, it is not so important to have stability in shamatha first.

Student: If one practices vipashyana, the mind is clearly seen as being empty. Why is that, if both appearance and mind are empty? Isn't vipashyana simply 'empty emptiness?'

Rinpoche: Experience is traditionally called the 'six collections of cognitions.' These are the perceptions of form, sound, smell, taste, texture and mental states. Mental cognition is the most important, the chief one. Once mental cognition is recognized to be empty, the other five, the five sense impressions, are automatically realized to be empty as well. To rephrase what Guru Rinpoche taught in the *Supplication in Seven Chapters*: No matter what you experience, whatever is perceived such as forms with your eyes, let it be, without holding on to a self-entity. Apparent yet empty, it is the body of the victorious ones. Whatever moves in the field of mind, all the different thoughts and emotions, allow these movements or thoughts to naturally dissolve. That is the mind of the victorious ones.

The most important is the frame of mind that does not grasp at these things. If the state of nongrasping mind is understood, then sense impressions or appearances are secondary.

Song of Karmapa

Student: What is there to look at when looking into our mind?

Rinpoche: Usually the words 'looked,' 'looking' or 'look' refer to an act of seeing or trying to see something, but in Mahamudra practice it means something different. In Mahamudra to 'look' means to remain mindful or alertly awake.

Tibetans have a saying: "Without relying on concepts, one cannot reach the ultimate truth. Without reaching the ultimate truth, one cannot attain nirvana." Right now we need words and conventional concepts to serve as a bridge to reach the other shore. Without conventional terminology we would be unable to comprehend the real meaning of the teachings. The word 'look' usually means doing something with your eyes such as examining a concrete object. The terms 'thinking' or 'contemplating' mean the mind has grasped a certain concept and is in the process of examining it.

In general the term 'meditation' refers to the process of visualizing a mental image or examining a topic, continuously holding it in mind. Here, however, the phrases 'looking into the nature' or 'meditating on the nature of mind' do not indicate a subject who meditates on or looks at an external object. Nor does it mean that our mind is focused on a mental object. Just as we use a vehicle to help us reach our destination, we can rely on a phrase like this as a vehicle to lead us into the deeper meaning. When we reach the other shore there is no point in carrying the boat around with us. Likewise, once we understand the ultimate truth we can let go of words. The words are like wrapping paper: by taking hold of them, we can uncover the hidden meaning.

The ultimate truth, the nature of mind, is beyond the reach of words and concepts. As long as we conceive of the ultimate truth as a mental object to accept, reject or label in a certain way, it will lie beyond our experience and remain mere intellectual understanding.

Song of Karmapa

Therefore, in order to truly experience the nature of mind we must abandon all speculation and assumptions about it. The ultimate truth can be experienced only when resting quietly in equanimity. When looking, be totally free of the idea of yourself looking, free of the idea of something being looked at and free from the conceptual act of looking. Only then is it possible to simply rest and 'see' the nature of mind.

The general Mahayana teachings refer to the nature of mind as the buddha nature, *sugatagarbha* in Sanskrit. According to the Third Turning of the Wheel of Dharma, it is called luminous Mahamudra or ground wisdom, basic wakefulness. What is this ground wisdom like? Since its nature is totally free from constructs it cannot be pigeon-holed or classified. In this state of ground wisdom free of confusion, the very concepts of samsara and nirvana are absent. Free from hope and fear, pleasure and pain, existing and nonexisting, being and not being, eternalism and nihilism, self and other and so forth, it lies totally beyond all words, labels, concepts, mental constructs and the confines of intellect. Its essence is the great emptiness: it is not composed of anything whatsoever, but by its cognizant nature everything can be perceived. Still, all that appears or is perceived is completely devoid of true existence, beyond the confines of arising, dwelling or ceasing. This empty and cognizant nature of mind is the uncompounded dharmadhatu within which the three kayas are spontaneously present. Ground wisdom is our own primordial nature, but as long as we are fettered by hope and fear or concepts of accepting and rejecting, this wisdom will remain obscured.

Buddhahood is nothing more than the simple attainment of stability in this ground wisdom through first recognizing and then training in it. We talk about ground Mahamudra, path Mahamudra, and fruition Mahamudra. Path Mahamudra means simply to maintain the continuity of our recognition of the ground

Song of Karmapa

wisdom which is inexpressible, indescribable and inconceivable. At the point of training in path Mahamudra, we can truly be called practitioners. Applying our experience of this ground wisdom as path, the fruition will be reached.

Student: How can objects be mind?

Rinpoche: That point is a little difficult to understand, and traditionally there has been a difference of opinion concerning the phrasing; whether we should say that perceived appearances are mind or that apparent objects are mind. One thing is certain, however: if there is no mind to perceive, then despite the existence of an object that could be experienced, there is no perception of it. The existence of a perceiving mind allows perception, so basically perception depends on the mind. Deluded experience is structured as a perceiving subject and the perceived object, and this duality we call perception. A kind of interdependence exists between the postulated subject and object.

Even without deep realization, through just thinking about this and applying what we have studied, we can reach the understanding that objects are objectless, that is, devoid of some self-existent entity or independent nature. This understanding is not enough, however. We must go further than understanding perceived objects to be empty, and realize the mind that perceives is also empty. Even without the wisdom resulting from meditation, we can still intellectually understand this through reasoning.

Student: When objects are seen to be objectless, and when observing the mind we see no mind, then dualistic fixation is naturally freed. You said this occurs spontaneously. Does this happen only through intellectual contemplation of those facts, or does it result from meditation?

Rinpoche: It results exclusively from meditation practice. A statement such as "When observing objects they are seen to be the mind, devoid of objects," is kind of shocking. It seems unreasonable, and we experience doubt. The objects we can see, hear, and touch are all around us, whereas the mind is here perceiving them, so how can objects and mind be the same? We might think of the mind as a thing that goes out to the objects, perceives them and then returns; or conversely, as a place where objects enter into and are then perceived, but it is a very difficult to conceive of objects and mind as identical.

The teachings, however, state that all perceptions are like reflections in a mirror. Whatever happens is a mental experience, just as in a dream. It is only because of our old habit of dualistic fixation that these experiences are held to be real and concrete. If someone entered our dream and said of our dreaming, "There are no real objects. Although they seem real, this is just a mental experience," we would feel just as shocked as we do when we hear this. The principle is the same. As long as we have not dissolved dualistic fixation, we will of course feel shocked. That is alright.

Student: What happens at the point of realizing that objects are just a dream and that mind is no mind? At some point, is there a realization of the true nature of the mind? Can you go deeper then?

Rinpoche: Realization is simply the collapse of dualistic fixation. That does not mean that with this collapse of duality we have no experience, that we do not perceive anything. It is not like a big blank. The qualities of the state of enlightenment, such as unimpeded knowledge, compassion and activity for the benefit of others, are still vividly present.

Student: Does that collapse come suddenly or over a period of time?

Song of Karmapa

Rinpoche: This depends on the type of person. There are the sudden and the gradual types. The sudden is like King Indrabodhi, whose realization and liberation were instantaneous. The other type must go step by step, learning and practicing more and more. This type of person must first recognize the mind nature, then train in it and finally attain stability. As one's fixation or grasping diminishes, so will the dualistic set-up of mind.

The example given for ordinary people is that of a bird which is totally helpless when it hatches from the egg. It sees the world, but without its mother's kindness and care it would be completely lost. It must be fed and nurtured so that it can slowly grow. Hatching from an egg symbolizes recognizing our nature. To do that the ordinary person must first learn, then contemplate and finally meditate. The master will introduce the student to his nature. Many methods for this exist, but the best introduction occurs in a moment of compassion and devotion. When unfabricated compassion and devotion are present in your mind, you can truly recognize the buddha nature, the view of Madhyamika, Dzogchen or Mahamudra.

The pointing-out instruction in itself is not sufficient for attaining buddhahood. Many people have been introduced to their nature but have not attained enlightenment. Having received the pointing-out instruction, you must train in order to grow accustomed to that recognition of mind essence. Develop strength in that recognition and become used to it, like the bird that slowly develops its wing power until it learns to fly and can one day finally take care of itself. When hungry or thirsty it can fly to get what it needs. That is the analogy for attaining stability. First recognize, next train in that recognition, and finally attain stability.

The mythological garuda exemplifies the person who takes the instantaneous approach. When hatched from the egg this bird is said to be totally developed and ready to fly, with the same prowess and power as its own mother. Because it is already perfected it need not go through any process of development. The garuda is the symbol of King Indrabodhi. He was a gifted person through training in past lives and so possessed the power of former practice. Otherwise he would have had to go through the steps of recognizing, training and attaining stability.

Student: What is the difference between enlightenment and liberation?

Rinpoche: In general, liberation means being free or liberated from the three realms of samsara, while enlightenment can be any stage from the first bhumi up to buddhahood. But you need to understand these terms in their individual contexts. They cannot be categorically defined.

Student: Could you say more about the luminosity mentioned in the verse about luminosity devoid of fixation? Experientially, what is luminosity like? How does it compare to the experience of clarity?

Rinpoche: In the phrase about luminosity devoid of fixation, 'luminosity' means a natural cognizance which is described as being free from fixation on the concepts of subject and object. It is unobscured by the darkness of ignorance, totally without any cover.

In the context of the three meditation experiences, clarity or sharpness of mind is the feeling that "Now I understand! I see clearly the viewpoints of all the philosophical schools!" During the experience of clarity all philosophical concepts are very clear in our minds.

When a moment of luminosity occurs, we call it the 'experience of clarity' if there is any clinging to it. If there is clinging we call it *nyam* or 'temporary experience,' connoting some attachment.

6

UNITY

The nature of all beings is always the enlightened state.
But, not realizing it, they wander endlessly in samsara.
Towards the countless sentient beings who suffer,
May overwhelming compassion arise in our minds.

This verse tells us how to embrace the practice of emptiness and compassion. In the first line, the statement that the nature of all beings is always the enlightened state means that buddha nature pervades all sentient beings. Just as milk has the potential to bring forth butter or sesame seeds oil, all sentient beings have this basic enlightened wakefulness without being aware of it. Their ignorance, which is their failure to realize this state, has caused them to wander in samsara since beginningless time. By failing to recognize the buddha nature they will continue to wander in samsara endlessly. Consider these sentient beings going through unending suffering; consider how they desire happiness but do not know how to achieve it and how they want to be free from pain without knowing how. If we think about this we will naturally feel compassion. So make the wish for overwhelming and genuine compassion to arise in our minds.

Usually three kinds of compassion are taught: compassion taking sentient beings as its focus, compassion taking the Dharma as focus, and the compassion which is beyond focus, which is the type referred to here. This compassion, which is free from any concepts and free from holding on to a certain object, is based on our understanding of the view of Mahamudra. It rises when the natural state of innate wakefulness dawns in our minds. The view of Mahamudra can occur in the moment of experiencing either deep-felt devotion to a qualified master whom we perceive as a buddha in person, or through sincere and unfabricated compassion towards sentient beings. The realization of the view is in itself endowed with compassion free from concepts, and is based on insight into how precious the understanding of the enlightened essence is and how many qualities it has. Seeing that sentient beings do not recognize this, we feel a spontaneous, unbearable compassion which does not need to be fabricated. Let us long for this overwhelming compassion to arise in our minds.

The play of overwhelming compassion being unobstructed,
In the moment of love the empty essence nakedly dawns.
May we constantly practice, day and night,
This supreme path of unity, devoid of errors.

Overwhelming means that from the core of our heart, unbearable compassion arises unobstructedly. In this moment, the view of emptiness, the nature of mind free from constructs, dawns nakedly in a way that is unmade and unspoiled. Thus we realize the inseparability of emptiness and compassion. There is no error in this; it is free of mistakes. Emptiness and compassion arise inseparably as means and knowledge. Make the aspiration never to separate day or night from this rapid and supreme path. Pray to become accustomed to the nature of mind, the inseparable emptiness and compassion which is the view of Mahamudra.

Song of Karmapa

The unity of means and knowledge, *prajna* and *upaya*, is the special quality of Secret Mantra. A bird needs both wings and intelligence to fly correctly. The means are its wings and the knowledge is its intelligence. If the bird is a little crazy or if its mind in somewhat confused, then although it has wings, instead of flying through an open window it might fly straight into a wall and hurt itself or even die. An intelligent bird knows exactly where the opening is and can arrive at its destination without being hurt. Similarly, when practicing Vajrayana, the main point is to unite means and knowledge. This means the unity of compassion and emptiness, through which we will definitely and easily be able to attain enlightenment.

The unity of means and knowledge is important at the time of ground and path as well as of fruition of Mahamudra. Ground Mahamudra is the inherent nature of wakefulness within oneself which is pointed out so that we can acknowledge or recognize it. Maintaining the continuity of that recognition is path Mahamudra. Fruition Mahamudra is the attainment of the last stage of the 'four times three' divisions of Mahamudra: the lesser, medium and higher stages for each of the four yogas (one-pointedness, simplicity, one taste and nonmeditation). The final stage is also called the dharmakaya throne of nonmeditation.

Each of these three aspects of Mahamudra includes the unity of compassion and emptiness. Compassion and emptiness are intrinsic to our nature in the state of the ground. On the path, our knowledge of emptiness is a help for the development of natural compassion, while compassion nurtures insight into emptiness. At the stage of fruition, the wakefulness that is the emptiness inseparable from compassion guarantees our total liberation from samsaric existence. Knowledge prevents us from circling in samsara, and compassion will not allow us to dwell in passive nirvana. This unified compassion and emptiness is expressed as the buddha activity which

Song of Karmapa

benefits beings by means of body, speech, mind, qualities and activities, so that both temporarily and ultimately, beings, as numerous as the sky is vast, are immensely benefited.

The qualities of compassion and wisdom are inherent to ground Mahamudra. Even a person who has not been introduced to Buddhist practice as the path still possesses knowledge in the sense of cognizance, the ability to perceive and to comprehend through the various functions of consciousness. We inherently also have love. Love need not be cultivated like compassion; we spontaneously love those who are close to us, our spouse, parents or children. Compared to the knowledge of knowing things as they are and the nonconceptual great compassion which arises at the level of buddhahood, our ordinary cognizance and love are very feeble and limited. Nonetheless they indicate our buddha nature, the potential to develop the supreme enlightened qualities.

Every sentient being possesses an enlightened essence which is the nature of mind, but the qualities of this buddha nature are not yet fully developed. The two obscurations cover our nature and hinder its development. For example, our eyes can be covered by an object the size of a thumb, but when uncovered, they can instantly perceive an entire valley or a vast landscape. Likewise, although we possess buddha nature with its numerous inherent qualities, it is obscured. Without practice, the qualities do not manifest. We may possess an enlightened nature, but still a full understanding of the basic nature of mind and of all knowable things remains beyond our experience. This is because the knowledge resulting from meditation experience has not yet been fully developed.

At this point, although we posses knowledge and compassion they are extremely limited. We can see what is on this side of the wall but have no idea of what is behind it. Even this limited knowledge is only partial.

Song of Karmapa

We assume that we know what we did yesterday, but if we ask ourselves, "What exactly did I do from when I woke up yesterday until I went to bed? What did I think of at all the different points of time?", we cannot possibly remember. Forgetting exactly what happened only a day ago, we can conclude that our knowledge is limited and imperfect. Ultimately, emptiness is basic wakefulness, but right now our understanding of emptiness is no more than a conceptual notion.

Likewise, although we have compassion and love, these are extremely limited and usually only shared with those we like. If we see somebody else suffering we say "How sad!" but it does not really bother us that much. If someone we do not like is suffering, we may even rejoice in their misfortune. However, if somebody whom we really love is suffering or if a close family member dies, we find it unbearable and suddenly an overwhelming compassion fills our hearts. When we are introduced to the nature of our mind and train in that, the power of knowledge and compassion gradually increases, the boundaries that set us apart from others break down and our perceptions will no longer be exclusive, but will become all-inclusive. Our qualities and activities as such will benefit infinite numbers of beings.

Questions and Answers

Student: Are compassion and emptiness and bliss and emptiness the same?

Rinpoche: If you realize emptiness exactly as it is, unmistakenly, then both compassion and the so-called 'great bliss' are inherently present. Different levels of teachings use different words like 'bliss and emptiness' or the 'wisdom that is the unity of compassion and emptiness' but actually they are all present in the same moment. All the different qualities such as wisdom, power, compassion and others are inherent once emptiness is correctly realized.

Song of Karmapa

Student: How does one feel compassion without a focus?

Rinpoche: The manifestation of objectless, nonconceptual compassion is like the reflection of the moon in water. The moon has no particular desire to be reflected, but due to the circumstances of there being the water and the moon, the reflection appears by itself. That is the effect of compassion beyond focus. This compassion arises naturally in the mind when you have the correct view.

Student: Rinpoche, sometimes when we experience pain we become so fixated on our own suffering that we lose perspective and lack compassion. We do not consider the fact that others might be suffering. Can you talk about how to help loosen this fixation and generate further compassion?

Rinpoche: There are different ways to approach that question. If one's own suffering is extremely strong, then one has no thought of anybody else at all. On the other hand, unless you yourself have suffered you will not even have the basis for understanding that others also suffer. You will not know what it is to suffer. If your suffering is moderate you may have the thought "Other people also suffer like this!" Through that experience you can feel some artificial or made-up compassion. However, without insight into egolessness and emptiness it is quite difficult to feel natural compassion for others. If we have no insight or if we do not practice the Dharma, then of course we will not think of others because we still consider ourselves to be most important. This is natural. For example, when a bus is going over a cliff everybody thinks of themselves, of how to get out of the window or the door as soon as possible. Very few would think "Let's all get out of here!" If the bus has not yet reached the cliff, we can take it easy and say "Let's all get out of this bus." But when the danger is real, when the situation is very intense, the most natural reaction for almost anybody is to think of himself first.

Song of Karmapa

It is very difficult to think of others when undergoing intense pain or despair. There is only one method at that moment and that is to recognize the empty nature, according to the oral instructions of our master. There is not much else to do other than to take painkillers. When we are experiencing less severe pain, we can indeed think of others and apply the general methods of mind-training, such as imagining that we are taking the suffering of others upon ourselves.

Student: Rinpoche, can you say something more about the relationship between compassion and emptiness? When compassion is fully manifested, how does insight into emptiness spontaneously arise?

Rinpoche: When we say that all sentient beings have buddha nature, we are not referring to inanimate objects such as rocks and tables. We mean that whatever has mind has buddha nature. Certain qualities, such as compassion, knowledge and ability, are inherent in this enlightened essence. These qualities are not present to the same extent at this point as they are at the time of complete enlightenment. Still, whatever has mind can to some extent perceive, can feel love and can act. That is because they have buddha nature. No matter how wicked a person might be, he can still love someone, maybe a close relative or a child. That is because of the nature of mind. That love originates from buddha nature.

Although we possess these qualities right now, their full potential is not manifest. The love, the knowledge and the ability we have is limited and partial. They are clouded by our disturbing emotions, our karma and our more subtle obscurations. When we realize the view of the unity of emptiness and compassion through practice, this potential for love, knowledge and ability will be immense, inconceivable and without any partiality whatsoever. Although the mind is empty, it still contains the basis for both faults and virtues. The virtues are the three potentials for love, knowledge and ability. The faults are the three poisons. We can say that in essence we are good, but in expression we can be good or evil. In other words, our nature is good but the way we express it can be either good or evil.

For example, think of a really good actor. During his daily life when he is not working, he may be a very gentle and peaceful person. But sometimes when working he is required to act as if he is in a great rage or in a mean and indecent manner. Yet in his heart he remains at peace. If he can act angry without really being angry it shows that he is a good actor. In this way the mind, though pure in essence, creates the three realms of samsara through the manifestations of the three poisons. These create the habits for wandering endlessly in samsara.

We may now understand that through insight into emptiness compassion can arise spontaneously, but not how insight can arise through the realization of compassion. The enemy of understanding emptiness is dualistic fixation. Once dualistic fixation collapses, we need not obtain insight from elsewhere. It is naturally manifest at that moment. Therefore at the instant of or just after feeling extremely strong love or compassion, there automatically comes a point where dualistic fixation falls apart. At that moment emptiness can be realized. It is possible to have a glimpse of recognition of our innate nature through love, meaning through compassion or devotion. That moment is dharmakaya, free from mental fabrication. We can glimpse something which lies completely beyond intellectual understanding, beyond the words of scholars and what can be read in books. This can happen not only through compassion but also through a moment of shock or fear.

Student: Is working on developing and realizing emptiness in meditation the most direct approach to realizing pure compassion?

Song of Karmapa

Rinpoche: First of all, people vary because of past mental patterns and different habitual tendencies. Even from an early age we have individual characters and dispositions. Some people are very gentle and peaceful in both behavior and attitude, while others are naturally more tough or short-tempered. Because of previous imprints made in our mind, we readily follow a certain pattern and are either gentle or short-tempered. Dharma teachings are meant to change these patterns. There are different methods to accomplish this, according to either the general teachings or the special, more direct instructions. The general teachings instruct us to try to be more mindful and more careful, to have more presence of mind and to be more disciplined in our actions. The special teachings include the development and completion stages of visualization, reciting mantra and resting in samadhi. Through these practices we become more gentle and compassionate and the realization of emptiness becomes easier.

We are taught that it is foolish to think of any other method for realizing emptiness besides gathering the accumulations, purifying obscurations and depending upon the blessings of a qualified master. Each of these aspects helps and is based on the others. The Kagyü lineage teaches that the preliminaries are even more profound than the main part of practice. This sounds odd. Why should something that is a preparation be more profound than that which follows? But if we really perform the preliminaries correctly, realizing the view in the main practice becomes easy. Without properly going through the preliminaries, having understanding in the main part of practice is very difficult. That is why the preliminaries are more profound and very important.

For example, when Milarepa met Marpa he had to undergo all kinds of trials and hardships without even a single word of teaching. That was a special case of a qualified student meeting a qualified master; neither of them had wrong appreciation of the other. Marpa did

Song of Karmapa

not simply put Milarepa to work because he considered him unsuitable; nor did Milarepa think "I am being misused for some trivial labor!" This link between qualified master and disciple enabled Milarepa to attain complete enlightenment within that very lifetime.

Student: What is compassion for? Isn't compassion a beginner's step on the path leading to nonduality? What is compassion ultimately?

Rinpoche: Enlightened compassion is nonconceptual; it does not hold an object in mind. Enlightenment comes after the collapse of dualistic fixation. To understand enlightened compassion we use the example of a person who is sleeping and has a nightmare. He sweats and kicks with his arms and legs and his heart is beating; he is having a terrible time. Then someone who is awake comes by, looks and says "How silly, how stupid to go through all this pain for no reason!" The sleeping person thinks his dream is real until the other person shakes him from the nightmare and awakens him. Likewise, a buddha who himself experiences no duality, no concept of 'I' and 'other', nonetheless perceives the confusion of others, their disturbing emotions and thoughts. This perception is the source from which spontaneous compassion arises.

Student: Is artificial compassion an obstacle to realizing emptiness?

Rinpoche: Usually when people enter a house they go by the staircase to get to the top floor. It is an easy, practical and comfortable way to get there without danger. If one can somehow jump onto the roof, that is fine, but it is more difficult. For most people, going step by step is easier. The methods used for realizing emptiness are usually devotion or compassion, gathering the accumulations and purifying the obscurations. Even though such methods are contrived or artificial, it is said that 'the artificial leads to the natural' when practiced correctly. The teachings explain that we should not remain involved with contrived, dualistic practices forever, but should gradually move beyond them. If we can jump to the roof, this is also fine.

Devotion is also an effective method to realize the view of Mahamudra. Dilgo Khyentse Rinpoche once said that Gampopa made a very special aspiration for future followers. He wished that whoever simply generated devotion towards Gampopa's house would have a glimpse of Mahamudra. It is very unusual that one should achieve understanding of Mahamudra just by feeling devotion towards a certain geographical direction, but actually this has happened for quite a few people.

When someone can learn music very easily and can play well without a lot of training, we call this a gift or a natural talent. The natural talent of the Kagyü lineage is devotion. In the moment of pure devotion one can glimpse and recognize the nature of Mahamudra. Otherwise devotion does not benefit that much. The master does not necessarily benefit from his disciples' devotion; he does not get rich from it or anything else. Nor would the students themselves benefit from feeling devotion if it did not facilitate recognizing the view of Mahamudra.

In a similar way compassion helps in recognizing the view of Mahamudra. The Indian mahasiddha Chandrakirti said: "I take refuge in compassion. Other people may take refuge in the Buddha, the Dharma, the Sangha, in Manjushri or Avalokiteshvara, but my object of refuge is compassion, because it is the source of all the buddhas." The arhants, who have realized the Hinayana teachings, attain their state by meditating on the Buddha's words. The Buddha's words are the source of the arhants' realization, but the buddhas themselves come from compassion. Genuine compassion is present within emptiness; they are inseparable. We can say that compassion is the true source of buddhahood, which is why Chandrakirti took refuge in it.

Song of Karmapa

In the moment of nonconceptual compassion, free from holding any focus, the view of emptiness is naturally present. Compassion and the view of emptiness are inseparable just as fire is inseparable from the flame.

7

Perfection

The eyes and superknowledges resulting from the power of practice,
The ripening of sentient beings, the cultivation of buddha realms,
And the perfection of aspirations to accomplish all enlightened qualities —
May we attain the buddhahood of having accomplished such ripening, cultivation, and perfection.

Learning, contemplation and meditation each lead to a slightly different result. Through study and thinking we gain intellectual understanding, but realization or true understanding of the nature as it is results only from meditation practice. Having received the pointing-out instruction and having correctly recognized the view of Mahamudra, what is derived from our meditation practice? Traditionally, one of the first results is called the 'five eyes and the six superknowledges.'

The five eyes are the physical eye, the divine eye, the eye of wisdom, the Dharma eye and the Buddha eye. Each possesses a wider vision than the previous one. That means that greater and greater distances can be seen. Simultaneously — not just one world but hundreds, then thousands, and finally one billion universes. This is the Buddha eye.

Song of Karmapa

The six kinds of superknowledges are divine sight, divine hearing, perception of the minds of others, perception of past lives, perception of death and transmigration of other beings, and the superknowledge of the exhaustion of defilement. 'Superknowledge' literally means what we commonly call clairvoyance, the ability to see what is usually hidden, or the ability to perceive very clearly in an extraordinary way. The Buddha has complete insight, full capacity. He is called 'the Knower of the Three Times.' We can only partially know the present moment. A fully enlightened being, however, perceives what has taken place in the past, what is occurring in the present, and what will happen in the future, all simultaneously and without obstruction. When we try to understand this we have a hard time believing it, and may even find it totally inconceivable. As ourselves do not experience such omniscience, we tend to doubt the possibility for someone else having it.

By the superknowledge of divine hearing, a buddha is able to distinguish clearly the individual sounds of both this and other worlds, without any confusion.

By the superknowledge of knowing the minds of others, a buddha can know the content of a certain sentient being's mind at this moment, as well as what he thought or felt yesterday and what he will think or feel tomorrow.

By the superknowledge of the recollection of former lives, a buddha can see where a certain being was reborn in a past life, which virtuous or unvirtuous actions he performed, what kind of karma he created, and the type of rebirth and state of joy or sorrow in which that karma will result.

The fifth superknowledge of death and transmigration differs from the recollection of former lives. By this superknowledge a buddha knows the circumstances of sentient beings' deaths; how and when they will die, and when and where they will be reborn.

Song of Karmapa

The sixth is the superknowledge of the exhaustion of defilements. This is the undefiled wisdom which clearly perceives the nature of things, whatever exists, both as they are and as how they appear.

There is also the superknowledge of miraculous powers of body, speech and mind. The miraculous powers of body include the ability to multiply one's form into countless forms, to condense countless forms into one, to appear or disappear at will, and to have such a magnificent form that people become delighted and magnetized by the mere sight of one.

By the miraculous powers of speech and mind a buddha's speech is never obscured or confused. He never makes mistakes or slips of the tongue. The power of his voice is such that it can be heard equally well by those sitting near or far away. In his mind there is never any confusion about what is being expressed; nor does he forget anything.

"May we attain the buddhahood of having accomplished ripening, cultivation, and perfection." The ripening is the ripening of sentient beings' karma; the cultivation is the cultivation of buddha realms; and the perfection is the aspiration to accomplish all enlightened qualities.

In essence these qualities come with the insight that increases with the growth of knowledge and compassion. For example, the shravakas can see a few lifetimes into the past whereas the bodhisattvas can see many lifetimes; the insight becomes progressively deeper. These are the qualities of our innate wisdom, the fruition of having practiced the inseparable unity of emptiness and compassion. These qualities arise when you truly realize the correct view.

Song of Karmapa
Questions and Answers

Student: Rinpoche, is the experience of Mahamudra meditation the same as bringing the winds into the central channel and melting the bodhichitta drops?

Rinpoche: There are three kinds of Mahamudra: sutra Mahamudra, tantra Mahamudra and essence Mahamudra. What you are talking about belongs to tantric Mahamudra. That kind of practice should be applied while maintaining the view of essence Mahamudra. Otherwise, merely practicing such yogic techniques without the Mahamudra view is not much different from being an ordinary person doing esoteric exercises. When applied in combination with the correct view of Mahamudra, however, they can very effectively accelerate progress. Essence Mahamudra does not mention the channels, winds or the Six Doctrines of Naropa much; it emphasizes only the view itself.

Student: If a person simultaneously experiences bliss, clarity and nonthought, is that real Mahamudra experience?

Rinpoche: Without fixation it is Mahamudra; with fixation it is not. If we were to describe the three kinds of experience, the experience of clarity could be described as perceiving night to be as bright as midday. The experience of nonthought could be described as feeling as if one were sitting in the sky, without even a physical body, which is why it is also called the empty experience. The experience of bliss could be described as having such a strong feeling of pleasure or ecstasy that we believe we have never known such rapture before. It is beyond description. The fault lies in clinging to these temporary experiences, because the clinging perpetuates cyclic existence. Having these experiences is good, but clinging to them is not.

The Mahamudra system is structured as four yogas which are each divided into three levels, making twelve stages. To accomplish all these, we must connect with a qualified master and proceed step by step. During the practice certain meditation experiences will occur. We need a proper guide in order to know what is what and to avoid sidetracks, errors and pitfalls. For instance, when we first experience clarity or nonthought we might think, "This is really it! It's what I've been waiting for! This is fantastic!" Without proper guidance we will cling to such an experience and try to cultivate it. A genuine master will say "Do not cling to it! Clinging to these experiences is the cause of error. Do not deliberately try to produce these experiences!"

We might think, "I need to have such-and-such experience!" and then sit and meditate in an attempt to get the experience. This way of practicing is wrong. Alternately, if these experiences occur we might think "This is bad, this is just a temporary meditation experience; I should get rid of it!" and try to suppress the experience. That is also wrong. The important thing is not to cling or fixate. As Tilopa told Naropa, "Son, you are not fettered by appearances but by attachment."

Student: Where is free will if the future is known to a buddha?

Rinpoche: This point is very difficult to understand. The Buddha can perceive all that is to come: the bad karma we will create tomorrow or the good action we will perform the day after. Even though the Buddha can perceive what will transpire, it is not the Buddha's function to do anything about it. The Buddha's activity is simply to show sentient beings how to practice the Dharma. It is taught that the Buddha cannot throw all sentient beings into a pure land or wash away their bad karma. Whether we do something or not is our free will, which is also perceived by the Buddha. This subject is very subtle.

Student: Are we able to change our future karma?

Song of Karmapa

Rinpoche: There are different kinds of karma, and also not everything is karma. If you start to think that everything is predestined, there is nothing we can do. Believing that our joys and sorrows are already laid out comes to exactly the same as thinking that God or the gods are creating everything.

Some things we cannot change. First of all we should know that the word karma means action, something that we willfully do, as well as the result of some action that is already done. Past karma cannot be changed, just as the shape of our face cannot be changed. It is the result of actions completed in the past. Our character and disposition is structured to some extent, and is difficult to change. On the other hand, with some actions, such as killing a worm or mosquito, we have an immediate and individual choice. We can choose whether or not to perform a present action. Whether we should eat a certain meal or sleep at a specific place is up to us right now. When we act intentionally, we create a karma and its result will follow, without fail. But not all karma is in our hands right now: some patterns linger on from past action. A small child can sometimes be naturally very kind. This results from being accustomed to kindness or compassion in a past life, and that pattern continues into the present. Other children who might like to kill animals have been habituated to killing in the past. Everything becomes a pattern which remains for some time in the mind. If as children we like a certain song, then hearing it when we are old makes us happy again.

We have all heard of the ten unvirtuous and the ten virtuous actions; we can easily count them and learn what they are. They are not very profound, but their effects are concrete and can be seen even in this life. Saving lives is said to result in an increased life span and less sickness. The result of stealing and robbing in a past life is always complaining in this life of not having enough of this or that. Some people get along very easily with others; no matter whom they are with, there are never any problems. That is because in the past they avoided slander and divisive talk. The reverse also happens; some people experience difficulty in getting on with others. In this way the ten virtuous or unvirtuous actions have both immediate and long-lasting effects.

You are also asking about the Buddha's capacity to perceive things which have not yet happened. Scholars often discuss the knowledge of an enlightened being: is it direct perception or does it result from inference? The special quality of a buddha is such that his knowledge is direct and not the result of thinking. Therefore we must say his perception of the three times is direct. Then does he have direct perception of the past, or of Buddha Dipamkara who is no longer here, or of the future Buddha Maitreya? If he perceives the past and future buddhas directly, then where are they right now? Does he see them or not? These things are discussed quite a bit.

Student: This is a two-part question. Can all sentient beings reach total enlightenment at some point? If so, does compassion exist or is it impermanent?

Rinpoche: The Buddha has said that if one tries, one can count all of the grains of sand in the River Ganges, but not the number of sentient beings. Because the number of all sentient beings cannot be counted, the time when all sentient beings will attain enlightenment cannot be estimated. We cannot say when this will happen, but neither can we say that it will not happen. Because we cannot say either of these, it is difficult to give an exact reply.

Actually, compassion is ultimately beyond the concepts of both permanence and impermanence, because that which thinks 'permanent or impermanent' is just conceptual mind, and conceptual mind is mistaken and cleared away at the time of enlightenment.

Song of Karmapa

Student: If compassion is attained and is without conceptual boundary or limitation, then is the person who has that attainment enlightened because no concept of enlightened or unenlightened remains?

Rinpoche: First of all, there is a certain Vajrayana practice used to purify our minds of impure perception which is known as cultivating the 'all-encompassing purity of all that appears and exists. But even after when one has purified one's mind through this practice, everything is perceived as pure only in one's own experience. Other confused beings still perceive things in an impure way. The state of enlightenment has two kinds of supreme knowledge: seeing the nature as it is and perceiving all that exists. Relative to the enlightened person himself, everything is pure: there is no suffering, no delusion, no ignorance. But relative to the experience of other people, which an enlightened being also perceives, there is suffering and all the samsaric realms do exist.

Student: Does the enlightened person perceive relative and absolute truth simultaneously?

Rinpoche: The qualities of an enlightened person are said to be beyond the grasp of ordinary thought, and the capacity of enlightened knowledge also belongs in that category. Think of a magician who can conjure up horses, elephants and human beings for others to perceive; he will also see them, but without fear or attachment. Those who perceive an illusory image of a beautiful man or woman may feel desire, or they may be terrified of an illusory tiger or an angry elephant. But the magician himself, knowing it is simply an apparition, will feel neither hope nor fear.

Likewise, an enlightened person perceives everything, but his experience is not colored by hope or fear. That does not mean that he is not aware of the hopes and fears of others. For example, children watching cartoons on television find them very enjoyable and may think them quite real. They are very happy and excited and need not eat or drink for many hours. Adults say "How foolish! Don't watch that, it doesn't make sense." But these same people might then become absorbed in watching a movie. They might say "How interesting! That is true!" But it is also fictitious. The experience depends upon the perceiver. Compared with children we think we are very smart, but are we really?

APPENDIX

Outline for the Aspiration of the Mahamudra of
True Meaning
According to the commentary
The Oral Teachings of Supreme Siddhas
by Situ Tenpey Nyinchey

The preparation for making the aspiration.
    Requesting the support remain as witness. Verse 1.

The aspiration itself.
    1. The general, dedicating the virtue towards complete enlightenment. Verse 2.
    2. The particular, making the aspiration. Verse 3-24.
        I. Aspiring for a perfect support for the path. Verse 3-4.
          i. The common. Verse 3.
          ii. The special. Verse 4.
        II. Aspiring for the intelligence that realizes the path. Verse 5.
        III. Aspiring for the unmistaken path itself. Verse 6.
        IV. Aspiring for the unmistaken way of practicing this path. Verse 7-24.
          i. Condensing the meaning to be understood. Verse 7.
          ii. The aspiration for practicing the meaning to be cultivated. Verse 8-24.
            A. Brief statement. Verse 8.
            B. Detailed explanation. Verse 9-24.
              a. Aspiring to the way the view cuts through misconceptions. Verse 9-14.
                1. Stated in brief. Verse 9.
                2. Unfolding this extensively. Verse 10-14.
                  I. Deciding that appearances are mind. Verse 10.
                  II. Establishing that mind is devoid of a self-nature. Verse 11-12.

Song of Karmapa

  i. Abandoning the extremes of existence and nonexistence. Verse 11.
  ii. Abandoning the extremes of being and not being. Verse 12.
 III. Showing that emptiness and interdependence are a unity without contradiction. Verse 13.
 IV. Instructing in the necessity of cutting through misconceptions about the ground by examining with discriminating knowledge. Verse 14.
b. Aspiring to the way meditation establishes the meaning of having cut through misconceptions. Verse 15-23.
1. Brief statement. Verse 15.
2. Detailed explanation. Verse 16-24.
 I. The yoga of shamatha and vipashyana. Verse 16-19.
  i. Shamatha. Verse 16.
  ii. Vipashyana. Verse 17-18.
   A. The actual explanation of vipashyana. Verse 17.
   B. Cutting through ground and root. Verse 18.
  iii. Stating the synonyms for the practice of shamatha and vipashyana as a unity. Verse 19.
 II. How experience and realization arise therefrom. Verse 20-21.
  i. Experience. Verse 20.
  ii. Realization. Verse 21.
 III. Stating the necessity for the practice of emptiness and compassion as a unity. Verse 22-23.
  i. Identifying compassion. Verse 22.
  ii. How compassion and emptiness are a unity. Verse 23.
 V. Aspiring for the fruition of having perfected the path. Verse 24.

Concluding the aspiration. Verse 25.